Low
FAT

OVER 80 DELICIOUS RECIPES

Nutritionist Fiona Hunter
Project Editor Elizabeth Yeates
Senior Designer Vanessa Hamilton
Designer Saskia Janssen
Senior Jacket Creative
Mark Penfound
Pre-Production Producer
Rebecca Fallowfield
Producer Konrad Kirkham
Special Sales Creative
Project Manager Alison Donovan

First published in Great Britain in 2015 by
Dorling Kindersley Limited,
80 Strand, London WC2R 0RL

Material previously published in
The Diabetes Cooking Book (2010),
The Gluten-free Cookbook (2012),
Family Kitchen Cookbook (2013), and
Complete Family Nutrition (2014)

Copyright © 2010, 2012, 2013, 2014, 2015
Dorling Kindersley Limited
A Penguin Random House Company
001 – 284061 – Mar/15

A CIP catalogue record for this book
is available from the British Library.
ISBN 978-0-2412-0052-0

Printed in China

All images © Dorling Kindersley Limited
For further information see: www.dkimages.com

A WORLD OF IDEAS:
SEE ALL THERE IS TO KNOW

Contents

Introduction

The food we eat can have an important effect on our health and wellbeing. A healthy diet will help protect against diseases, increase resistance to colds and other infections, boost energy levels, help combat stress, and improve physical and mental performance. Eating well doesn't have to be difficult – you just need to know the key foods to include in your diet.

THE RECIPE FOR A HEALTHY DIET

The three key ingredients in a healthy diet are variety, balance, and moderation.

Variety

Your body needs over 40 different nutrients to accomplish every bodily task. No single food or food group – fruit and vegetables, proteins, carbohydrates, dairy, and fats – can provide all the essential nutrients, which is why you need to choose a variety of foods. The greater the variety of foods in your diet, the more chance you have of getting the key nutrients you need.

Balance

Ensure you eat the right amount of food from all of the food groups (see *Healthy eating in a nutshell*, right). Eating a balanced diet will provide your body with the energy and nutrients it needs. It will also keep your weight within its ideal range.

Moderation

Healthy eating doesn't mean giving up the foods you enjoy, it is simply a question of learning to eat them in moderation. By choosing natural and unprocessed foods and using cooking methods that use little or no fat (steaming and grilling for example), you can still enjoy all your favourite foods.

HEALTHY EATING IN A NUTSHELL

Eat a varied diet containing all of the food groups. Experts recommend the following guidelines:

• **Fruit, vegetables, and plant-based food:** eat plenty of fruit and vegetables and other plant-based foods, such as beans and pulses. You should have at least five portions a day, making up a third of your daily food intake.

• **Protein:** this includes meat, poultry, fish, and eggs. Aim to eat two to three small portions every day and always choose lean cuts of meat, with any excess fat removed.

• **Carbohydrates:** the body needs starchy (also known as complex) carbs to convert into energy. These include potatoes, cereals, and grains, plus bread and pasta. Eat at least five portions a day and choose wholegrains where possible.

• **Dairy:** milk, yogurt, and cheese provide us with essential calcium and other vitamins and minerals. Eat two to three low-fat portions a day.

• **Fats:** these should be eaten in moderation. Some fats are better than others: avoid saturated and trans fats, which are found in processed foods, as they clog arteries with cholesterol. Healthier unsaturated fats (poly- and monounsaturated) can reduce cholesterol levels, so it is always better to eat and use these. They are found in rapeseed oil and avocados.

HOW TO USE THE RECIPES

Icons These appear at the top of every recipe and advise on preparation and cooking times.

Cook's tip These give useful advice on how to adapt a recipe or how to prepare a certain ingredient.

Nutrition boxes The nutritional breakdown provides the amount of calories, protein, fat, carbohydrates, and sugar per serving.

A low-fat diet

Fat is the most debated and misunderstood food group. Contrary to popular belief, it is essential in our diet; it cushions and protects the vital organs, provides energy stores, and helps insulate the body. The problem is that too many of us are eating too much of the wrong sorts of fat, which increases our susceptibility to numerous health issues.

FAT: FRIEND OR FOE?

There are three types of fat: saturated, monounsaturated, and polyunsaturated. All three types are made up of smaller units called fatty acids, which determine how the fats we ingest behave in our body.

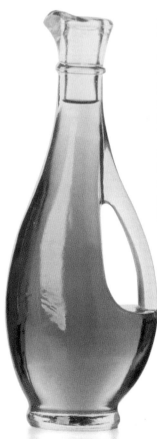

Saturated fats

These are found in dairy products (cheese, crème fraîche, yogurt, milk, cream, ice cream), lard, fatty cuts of meat and meat products like sausages and burgers, pastry, cakes, biscuits, coconut, and palm oil. A diet high in saturated fats can raise levels of "bad" cholesterol in the blood, which can cause narrowing of the arteries and increase the risk of heart attacks and stroke, and reduce levels of "good" cholesterol. Make sure that you eat foods containing saturated fats only in moderation.

Monounsaturated fats

These are found in olive, walnut, and rapeseed oil, as well as nuts, seeds, and avocados. They are what nutritionists call "heart friendly" fats because they help to lower cholesterol.

Polyunsaturated fats

These can be split into two groups, based on their chemical structure:

• **Omega-6 fats:** these are found in vegetable oils and margarines, such as sunflower, safflower, corn, and soya bean oil. Omega-6 fatty acids are essential for growth, cell structure, and boosting the immune system.

• **Omega-3 fats:** these are found mainly in oil-rich fish, such as salmon, fresh tuna, mackerel, and sardines, as well as in linseeds (flax), and rapeseed oil. They help to protect the heart by reducing the likelihood of blood clots, lowering blood pressure, and by encouraging the muscles lining the artery walls to relax, which improves blood flow to the heart. Recent research suggests that low levels of omega-3 fats in the blood may contribute to depression, antisocial behaviour, and schizophrenia.

It's important to have a balance of omega-3 and omega-6 fats in the diet. Most of us consume too many omega-6 fats and not enough omega-3 fats.

HOW LOW IS LOW?

Studies show we are eating too much of the wrong type of fat. It is estimated that 80% of adults in the UK currently eat more than the recommended amount of saturated fat and 50% eat more than the recommended total amount of fat (see below).

Gram for gram, fat contains twice as many calories as protein or carbohydrate, which means that foods that contain a high quantity of fat will also contain a high number of calories. A high-fat diet (particularly one that contains a lot of saturated fats), is known to increase the risk of serious health issues including heart disease, stroke, and certain types of cancer.

The recommended daily allowance of fat for women is 70g total fat, of which only 20g should be saturated fat. For men, the daily allowance is 90g total fat of which 30g should be saturated fat. When following a low-fat diet, you should consume no more than 36g per day, of which only 5g or less should be saturated fat.

Choosing healthier proteins

Meat and meat products are one of the major sources of fat, especially saturated fat, but some are better than others; turkey and chicken breast (without skin) are lower-fat options, as is pork loin.

Fish and shellfish are preferable to meat, as most contain less than five per cent fat, and this fat is mainly polyunsaturated. Try eating lobster, prawns, scallops, halibut, tuna, or salmon. Oily fish, such as herring, mackerel, sardines, and anchovies, are higher in fat but these are primarily omega-3 fats (see above).

BREAKFAST AND BRUNCH

Baked beans

Commercial baked beans often contain gluten, but
making your own is surprisingly easy.

INGREDIENTS

1 tbsp olive oil

1 onion, finely chopped

salt and freshly ground
    black pepper

2 garlic cloves, finely chopped

1 tsp ground allspice

1 tsp paprika

1 tbsp tomato purée

1 tsp Dijon mustard

1 tbsp black treacle

600ml (1 pint) passata

2 x 400g cans haricot beans,
    drained and rinsed

toast or grilled streaky bacon
    (fat trimmed), to serve

SERVES 4   **PREP** 10 MINS   **COOK** 40 MINS

1 Heat the oil in a large pan, add the onion, season with salt and
pepper, and cook gently for about 2–3 minutes until translucent;
do not allow to brown. Stir through the garlic, allspice, paprika,
tomato purée, and mustard and cook for a few seconds.

2 Now add the treacle and 2 tablespoons passata, stir well, cook for
a few minutes, then add the remaining passata and bring to the
boil. Reduce to a low heat and simmer for about 20–30 minutes.

3 Tip in the beans, stir, and cook for a further 15 minutes or until
thickened. Taste and season some more if required. Serve with
toast or grilled streaky bacon.

Cook's tip: You can also use cannellini beans or butter beans as an alternative.

Nutrition data per serving

Energy	210kcals/889kJ
Carbohydrate	34g
of which sugar	5.3g
Fat	4g
of which saturates	0.7g
Salt	0.2g
Fibre	12g

Breakfast smoothie

Smoothies are a great way to boost your intake of fruit, and this sustaining recipe will give you a shot of calcium as well as vitamins and minerals.

INGREDIENTS

2 small, ripe bananas

500ml (16fl oz) semi-skimmed milk

3 tbsp oatmeal

100g (3½oz) fresh raspberries

150ml (7fl oz) fat-free Greek yogurt

½ tsp ground cinnamon

SERVES 2 **PREP** 5 MINS

1 Cut the bananas into small chunks and place in a blender along with the remaining ingredients. Blend at high speed for 1–2 minutes or until smooth.

2 Pour into two glasses and drink immediately.

Nutrition data per serving

Energy	336kcals/1420kJ
Carbohydrate	52g
of which sugar	29g
Fat	6g
of which saturates	3g
Salt	0.3g
Fibre	4g

Autumn fruit compote

When the temperature is cooler, try this seasonal fruit salad
for breakfast or dessert, served hot or cold.

INGREDIENTS

100g (3¹/₂oz) dried apples
100g (3¹/₂oz) dried figs
100g (3¹/₂oz) dried prunes
1 cinnamon stick
¹/₂ vanilla pod, halved
    lengthways
finely grated zest and
    juice of 1 orange
1 tbsp demerara sugar
Greek-style yogurt or
    porridge, to serve

SERVES 4   **PREP** 10 MINS,
                    PLUS SOAKING   **COOK** 15 MINS

1 Place all the dried fruits in a mixing bowl. Add the cinnamon, vanilla pod, and orange zest and juice. Pour in 200ml (7fl oz) of boiling water. Cover the bowl and set aside overnight.

2 In the morning, transfer the contents of the bowl to a saucepan. Add the sugar and 150ml (5fl oz) of cold water and bring to the boil.

3 Reduce the heat and simmer very gently, uncovered, for 15 minutes. Remove the vanilla pod and cinnamon stick. Serve with a dollop of Greek-style yogurt, or with porridge.

Nutrition data per serving

Energy	165kcals/703kJ
Carbohydrate	38g
of which sugar	38g
Fat	trace
of which saturates	trace
Salt	trace
Fibre	8g

Savoury breakfast muffins

These unusual muffins add a savoury twist
to a weekend breakfast or brunch.

INGREDIENTS

350g (12oz) self-raising
  flour, sifted
1 tsp baking powder
200g (7oz) grated Lancashire
  cheese
100g (3½oz) thick-cut ham,
  finely diced
4 spring onions, finely sliced
1 tsp smoked paprika
freshly ground black pepper
350ml (12fl oz) whole milk
1 egg, lightly beaten

MAKES 12   **PREP** 10 MINS   **COOK** 25 MINS

1 Preheat the oven to 180°C (350°F/Gas 4). In a large bowl, mix
together all the dry ingredients until they are well combined.

2 Mix together the milk and egg. Make a well in the centre of the
dry ingredients and pour the milk mixture in, incorporating it
gradually to make a thick batter.

3 Line a 12-hole muffin tin with paper muffin cases, then divide
the batter between them.

4 Bake in the middle of the oven for 25 minutes until the muffins
are well risen and a skewer comes out clean. Transfer to a wire
rack to cool for 5 minutes. Serve warm.

Nutrition data per serving

Energy	200kcals/835kJ
Carbohydrate	22g
of which sugar	2g
Fat	8g
of which saturates	4g
Salt	0.9g
Fibre	1g

Lemon and poppy seed muffins

These light and lemony muffins make a pleasant, refreshing change
when baked for a weekend breakfast or brunch.

INGREDIENTS

250g (9oz) self-raising flour
1 tsp baking powder
¼ tsp salt
125g (4½oz) caster sugar
finely grated zest of 1 lemon
1 heaped tsp poppy seeds
100ml (3½fl oz) whole milk
100ml (3½fl oz) plain yogurt
3½ tbsp sunflower oil
1 large egg, lightly beaten
2 tbsp lemon juice

For the glaze
2 tbsp lemon juice
150g (5½oz) icing sugar
finely grated zest of 1 lemon

MAKES 12   **PREP** 10 MINS   **COOK** 15 MINS

1 Preheat the oven to 200°C (400°F/Gas 6) and line a 12-hole muffin tin with paper muffin cases. Sift the flour, baking powder, and salt into a large bowl. Use a balloon whisk to mix through the sugar, lemon zest, and poppy seeds.

2 Measure the milk, yogurt, and oil into a jug, then add the egg and lemon juice and beat it all together thoroughly. Pour the liquid into the centre of the dry ingredients and mix with a wooden spoon until just amalgamated. Be careful not to over-mix.

3 Divide the mixture equally between the muffin cases and bake in the middle of the preheated oven for 15 minutes until the muffins are lightly brown and well risen. Remove from the oven and allow them to cool in the tin for 5 minutes before transferring to a wire rack to cool completely.

4 For the glaze, mix the lemon juice and icing sugar to a thin icing, drizzle it over the muffins, and sprinkle them with lemon zest

Nutrition data per serving

Energy	209kcals/886kJ
Carbohydrate	38g
of which sugar	24g
Fat	5g
of which saturates	1g
Salt	0.4g
Fibre	1g

Banana and oatmeal muffins

These muffins are a tasty and healthy choice for a late leisurely brunch; delicious eaten when they're still warm.

INGREDIENTS

160g (5³/₄oz) plain flour
1 tsp bicarbonate of soda
1 tsp baking powder
1 tsp ground cinnamon
100g (3¹/₂oz) oatmeal
50g (1³/₄oz) chopped walnuts (optional)
110g (3³/₄oz) butter, softened, plus extra for greasing (if using a tin)
100g (3¹/₂oz) demerara sugar
2 eggs, lightly beaten
3 ripe bananas, mashed
120ml (4fl oz) whole milk

MAKES 12   **PREP** 20 MINS   **COOK** 20 MINS

1 Preheat the oven to 190°C (375°F/Gas 5). Place 12 paper muffin cases in a 12-hole muffin tin, or simply place the cases on a baking tray, or grease a 12-hole muffin tin with butter.

2 Sift the flour, bicarbonate of soda, baking powder, cinnamon, and oatmeal into a large bowl. Tip in any bran left in the sieve. Add the walnuts (if using). Stir well.

3 Place the butter and demerara sugar in a separate mixing bowl and cream together, using an electric hand-held whisk, until very light and fluffy. (This could take as much as 5 minutes, so be patient!) Add the eggs and mix well. Stir in the bananas and milk.

4 Pour the wet mixture into the dry and stir to combine. Do not over-mix or the muffins will be heavy. Divide the mixture between the paper cases or muffin tin holes.

5 Bake for 20 minutes (start checking after 15), or until a cocktail stick inserted into a muffin comes out clean. Transfer to a wire rack to cool.

Nutrition data per serving

Energy	192kcals/811kJ
Carbohydrate	29g
of which sugar	14g
Fat	6g
of which saturates	1.5g
Salt	0.4g
Fibre	2g

Sweet potato and rosemary rolls

The gentle, aromatic scent of rosemary makes these rolls
something special. Eat them warm, with butter.

INGREDIENTS

300g (10oz) plain flour,
  plus extra for dusting
100g (3½oz) wholemeal
  self-raising flour
1 tsp bicarbonate of soda
½ tsp fine salt
freshly ground black pepper
140g (5oz) sweet potato,
  finely grated
1 tsp finely chopped
  rosemary leaves
250ml (9fl oz) buttermilk

MAKES 8   **PREP** 20 MINS   **COOK** 20-25 MINS

1 Preheat the oven to 220°C (425°F/Gas 7). Line a baking sheet with
baking parchment. In a bowl, mix the flours, bicarbonate of soda,
salt, and pepper. Mix in the sweet potato and rosemary.

2 Stir in the buttermilk, bringing the mixture together to form
a loose dough. Turn it out onto a floured surface and knead for
2 minutes to form a smooth dough. You may need a little more flour.

3 Divide into 8 equal pieces, and shape each into a tight round.
Flatten the tops and cut a cross in the centres with a sharp knife
to help them rise in the oven.

4 Place the rolls on the lined baking tray. Cook in the middle of the
oven for 20–25 minutes until the rolls are well risen and golden
brown. Transfer to a wire rack and allow to cool for at least 10 minutes
before serving.

Nutrition data per serving	
Energy	195kcals/829kJ
Carbohydrate	39g
of which sugar	3.5g
Fat	1g
of which saturates	0.5g
Salt	1.1g
Fibre	3.5g

Buckwheat, oat, and apple pancakes

Buckwheat produces dark, nutty pancakes, which are lightened by the addition of grated apple. Serve them with a drizzle of maple syrup or fruit compote.

INGREDIENTS

50g (1³/₄oz) rolled oats

50g (1³/₄oz) buckwheat flour or spelt flour

2 tbsp caster sugar

1 tsp baking powder

1 tsp cinnamon

125ml (4¹/₄fl oz) buttermilk or whole milk

1 egg, separated

¹/₂ tsp vanilla extract

1 large apple, peeled and roughly grated (about 100g/3¹/₂oz of grated apple)

1 tbsp butter, plus extra if needed

maple syrup or fruit compote, to serve

MAKES 8   **PREP 10 MINS**   **COOK 10 MINS**

1 Process the oats in a food processor to a fine flour consistency. Transfer to a bowl and add the buckwheat flour, sugar, baking powder, and cinnamon. Mix well to combine.

2 Whisk together the buttermilk, egg yolk, and vanilla extract. In a separate bowl, whisk the egg white to form soft peaks. Make a well in the centre of the flour mixture, and whisk in the milk mixture. Beat until smooth. Fold the grated apple and the whisked egg white into the batter.

3 Melt the butter in a large, non-stick frying pan over a medium heat. Pour small ladlefuls of batter into the pan and spread to about 7cm (3in) in diameter. Cook each pancake for 2–3 minutes. Turn them over and cook for a further 1–2 minutes, until cooked through.

Nutrition data per serving

Energy	97kcals/406kJ
Carbohydrate	15g
of which sugar	6g
Fat	3g
of which saturates	1g
Salt	0.2g
Fibre	1g

Apple and oat pancakes

These little pancakes are a perfect treat for the weekend. The oats used in the mixture provide soluble fibre and help to slow down the absorption of carbohydrate.

INGREDIENTS

125g (4½oz) plain flour
1 tsp baking powder
75g (2½oz) porridge oats
2–3 tbsp caster sugar
pinch of ground cinnamon
2 eggs, separated
284ml carton buttermilk
2 medium apples
sunflower oil, for frying

MAKES 12   **PREP** 10 MINS   **COOK** 15 MINS

1 Sift the flour into a large bowl and mix with the baking powder. Stir in the oats, sugar, and cinnamon. Make a well in the centre and beat in the egg yolks and buttermilk to make a thick batter (it should have the consistency of heavy cream).

2 Core the apples, coarsely grate the flesh, and stir into the batter mixture. Whisk the egg whites until stiff but not dry and fold into the batter.

3 Heat a griddle pan or large heavy-based non-stick frying pan over a moderate heat. Add a tiny drop of oil to the hot pan. When the pan is hot, drop a heaped dessertspoon of the batter into the pan and flatten slightly with the back of the spoon so that the pancakes are about 10cm (4in) in diameter and about 5mm (¼in) thick.

4 Cook for 2 minutes or until bubbles start to break on the surface and the pancakes are firm enough to flip. Flip and cook for 1–2 minutes more, until they feel springy when prodded. Transfer to a warm oven while you cook the rest, adding more oil as necessary. Try these with fresh summer fruits and low-fat Greek yogurt, or with your own favourite topping.

Nutrition data per serving

Energy	100kcals/418kJ
Carbohydrate	14g
of which sugar	5.5g
Fat	2g
of which saturates	0.5g
Salt	0.17g
Fibre	1.1g

Classic American buttermilk pancakes

You can make these pancakes with whole milk instead,
but using tangy buttermilk makes them lighter.

INGREDIENTS

225g (8oz) self-raising flour, sifted
1 tsp baking powder
25g (scant 1oz) caster sugar
150ml (5fl oz) buttermilk
100ml (3½fl oz) whole milk
2 large eggs, lightly beaten
1 tsp vanilla extract
25g (scant 1oz) butter, melted
    and cooled, plus extra for
    frying, plus extra to serve
maple syrup, to serve

MAKES 20   **PREP** 15 MINS   **COOK** 10-12 MINS

1 Use a large balloon whisk to mix together the flour, baking powder, and sugar in a large bowl.

2 Measure the buttermilk and milk into a jug, then add the eggs and vanilla extract and whisk it well. Whisk in the cooled, melted butter.

3 Make a well in the centre of the flour mixture and slowly whisk in the milk mixture, using the whisk to bring in the flour gradually from the edges of the well, until it has formed a thick batter.

4 Pour the batter back into the jug. Heat a knob of butter in a large, non-stick frying pan and pour out as many 8–10cm (3¼–4in) pancakes as will fit comfortably in the pan. Fry them for 2 minutes on each side, turning when the edges are set and bubbles appear and pop on the surface. When they are cooked, keep them warm on a plate under a clean tea towel while you fry the rest.

Nutrition data per serving	
Energy	75kcals/317kJ
Carbohydrate	10g
of which sugar	2g
Fat	3g
of which saturates	1.5g
Salt	0.3g
Fibre	0.5g

Sweet potato cakes with onion seeds

Onion seeds add a subtle spice to the mixture and cut through
the richness of sweet potato. These make a lower-carb
option to regular potato pancakes.

INGREDIENTS

2 medium sweet potatoes,
   skin on
2 eggs, lightly beaten
175g (6oz) rice flour
3 tsp baking powder
$^1/_2$ tsp freshly grated nutmeg
1 tbsp black onion (nigella) seeds
salt and freshly ground
   black pepper
knob of butter, for frying
bacon and grilled tomatoes,
   to serve

SERVES 6   **PREP** 30 MINS   **COOK** 20-30 MINS

1 Cook the whole potatoes in a pan of salted water for about 15–20 minutes or until soft, then drain. When cool enough to handle, peel and mash until smooth. Add the eggs and mix until well incorporated. Set aside.

2 Sift the flour and baking powder into a bowl, add the nutmeg, and mix. Add to the sweet potato and stir gently to mix well. Don't overwork the mixture or it will become sloppy. Stir in the onion seeds and season.

3 In a non-stick frying pan, heat a little butter over a medium heat until it is foaming, then add 1 heaped tablespoon of the potato mixture and flatten slightly with a palette knife. Cook for 4–5 minutes until the underside becomes golden, then flip, and cook the other side for the same time or until browned. Repeat to use up the batter. Serve with bacon and grilled tomatoes.

Nutrition data per serving

Energy	210kcals/880kJ
Carbohydrate	36g
of which sugar	4g
Fat	5g
of which saturates	1.6g
Salt	0.8g
Fibre	2g

Masala dosa

These spicy vegan pancakes, made from ground lentils and rice,
are traditionally served for breakfast in southern India.

INGREDIENTS

175g (6oz) basmati rice
60g (2oz) urad dal
1 tsp fenugreek seeds
salt
vegetable oil, for frying

For the potato filling
2 tbsp vegetable oil
1 onion, finely chopped
1 green chilli, deseeded and
    chopped
1 garlic clove, finely chopped
2.5cm (1in) piece of fresh root
    ginger, grated
2 tsp black mustard seeds
$\frac{1}{4}$ tsp turmeric
6 dried curry leaves
450g (1lb) potatoes, cubed
zest and juice of $\frac{1}{2}$ lemon
2 tbsp finely chopped fresh
    coriander

For the dipping sauce
30g (1oz) fresh coriander
1 small tomato
$\frac{1}{2}$ green chilli, deseeded
juice of 1 lemon
$\frac{1}{2}$ tsp caster sugar

SERVES 6

**PREP 20 MINS,
PLUS SOAKING**

COOK 40-50 MINS

1 Place the rice, dal, and fenugreek seeds in a large bowl, cover with cold water, and soak for 6–8 hours or overnight. Drain and coarsely grind in a food processor with a pinch of salt. Add 300ml (10fl oz) cold water and process to a smooth batter the consistency of thin cream.

2 For the spicy potato filling, heat the oil in a medium pan and fry the onion for 4 minutes or until soft. Add the chilli, garlic, ginger, mustard seeds, turmeric, and curry leaves and cook for 30 seconds or until the mustard seeds start to pop. Add the potatoes, lemon zest and juice, a good pinch of salt, and 250ml (8fl oz) water. Bring to the boil, cover, and simmer for 15–20 minutes until tender. Remove the lid and simmer until soft and breaking up. Stir in the coriander and keep warm. For the sauce, place all the ingredients with a pinch of salt in a food processor and whizz to a rough paste.

3 Heat 1 teaspoon oil in a small frying pan. Cover the pan with a ladleful of batter and cook over medium heat for 2–3 minutes. Flip and cook for another 1–2 minutes. Keep warm. Repeat to make 6 pancakes. Divide the potato filling between the pancakes, fold over, and serve with the sauce.

Nutrition data per serving

Energy	250kcals/1049kJ
Carbohydrate	40g
of which sugar	2.3g
Fat	6g
of which saturates	0.7g
Salt	0.3g
Fibre	3g

LUNCH

Tomato, bean, and pasta soup

If you make this ahead of time, you may need to add more water
when reheating, as it thickens on standing.

INGREDIENTS

1 tbsp olive oil
1 onion, finely chopped
1 carrot, finely chopped
2 garlic cloves, finely chopped
2 x 400g cans chopped tomatoes
400g can butterbeans, drained
and rinsed
400g can cannellini beans,
drained and rinsed
450ml (15fl oz) vegetable stock
salt and freshly ground
black pepper
75g (2½oz) mini dried
pasta shapes
1 tsp finely chopped basil leaves
grated Cheddar cheese, to serve

SERVES 4-6   **PREP** 15 MINS   **COOK** 45-50 MINS

1 Heat the oil in a large saucepan over a medium-low heat. Add the
onion and carrot and fry for about 5 minutes, stirring occasionally,
until softened, but not browned. Add the garlic and fry for a further
minute, or until it is fragrant, but not browned.

2 Add the tomatoes, beans, and stock. Season, cover, and simmer
gently for 25 minutes, stirring occasionally.

3 Add the pasta and cook the soup for a further 15 minutes, stirring
occasionally so it does not stick to the pan. Add a little more water
if the soup seems to be becoming too thick.

4 Add the basil and stir it through, then ladle the soup into warmed
bowls and sprinkle with grated cheese, to serve.

Cook's tip: Cooking your own pulses is cheaper and tastier. For every 400g can,
soak 100g of dried pulses overnight. Cook according to the packet instructions
(without salt) before adding them to the soup.

Nutrition data per serving	
Energy	242kcals/1024kJ
Carbohydrate	38g
of which sugar	10g
Fat	4.5g
of which saturates	0.5g
Salt	1.6g
Fibre	11.5g

Aduki bean and vegetable soup

A wholesome mix of goodness, these red beans
have a meaty texture to them.

INGREDIENTS

1 tbsp olive oil
1 red onion, finely chopped
2 garlic cloves, finely chopped
3 celery stalks, finely diced
3 carrots, peeled and finely diced
1 bay leaf
1 tbsp yeast extract (Marmite)
2 x 410g cans aduki beans,
   drained and rinsed
750ml (1¼ pints) vegetable stock
freshly ground black pepper

SERVES 4   **PREP** 10 MINS   **COOK** 35 MINS

1 Heat the oil in a large saucepan, then add the onion and cook on a low heat for 2–3 minutes or until soft. Stir in the garlic, celery, carrot, and bay leaf and continue to cook for a further 10 minutes until the vegetables begin to soften.

2 Stir through the yeast extract, add the beans and the stock, and bring to the boil. Reduce the heat and simmer gently for 20 minutes, adding more stock if needed.

3 Remove the bay leaf and season to taste with black pepper (you are unlikely to need salt, as the yeast extract can be salty). Spoon into bowls and serve with chunks of wholemeal bread.

Nutrition data per serving

Energy	388kcals/1632kJ
Carbohydrate	41g
of which sugar	10g
Fat	6.5g
of which saturates	2g
Salt	0.5g
Fibre	11g

Chicken noodle soup

This simple healthy soup is perfect
for grey winter days.

INGREDIENTS

2 tbsp olive oil

1 onion, finely chopped

1 leek, white part only, finely
  chopped

1 celery stick, finely chopped

2 carrots, finely chopped

1.2 litres (2 pints) chicken stock

200g (7oz) cooked chicken,
  shredded, or the meat from
  making chicken stock

150g (5½oz) soup noodles, such
  as vermicelli

salt and freshly ground black
  pepper

2 tbsp finely chopped
  flat-leaf parsley leaves,
  to serve (optional)

SERVES 4   **PREP** 20 MINS   **COOK** 20 MINS

1 Heat the oil in a large saucepan. Add the vegetables and fry over a
  medium heat for 5–7 minutes until softened, but not browned.

2 Add the stock and bring to the boil. Reduce the heat to a gentle
  simmer and cook for about 10 minutes, until the vegetables are soft.

3 Add the chicken and noodles and continue to cook until the noodles
  are ready (follow the package instructions). Check the seasoning,
  add the parsley (if using), and serve.

Nutrition data per serving

Energy	359kcal/1503kJ
Carbohydrate	35g
of which sugar	5.5g
Fat	8g
of which saturates	1.5g
Salt	0.9g
Fibre	3g

Minted split pea and tomato soup

This soup is full of goodness, warming, and nutritious,
as well as being very delicious.

INGREDIENTS

2 tbsp olive oil
1 large onion, finely chopped
2 garlic cloves, crushed
400g can chopped tomatoes
1 litre (1¾ pints) vegetable stock
250g (9oz) dried split peas
2 tsp dried mint
salt and freshly ground
    black pepper

SERVES 6   **PREP** 10 MINS   **COOK** 1 HR

1 Heat the oil in a large, heavy-based saucepan with a lid. Fry the onion for 5 minutes over a medium heat, until it has softened, but not browned. Add the garlic and cook for a further minute.

2 Add the rest of the ingredients, season well, and bring to the boil. Reduce the heat to a low simmer and cook for up to 1 hour, stirring occasionally, or until the peas have softened. Keep an eye on it: start checking after 30 minutes, as different batches of split peas cook at varying rates.

3 Blend the soup, either in a blender or using a hand-held blender. You can process until completely smooth, or leave it a little chunky if you prefer.

Nutrition data per serving

Energy	229kcals/954kJ
Carbohydrate	26g
of which sugar	4g
Fat	5g
of which saturates	0.7g
Salt	0.6g
Fibre	4.5g

Three-grain salad

A real good-for-you, wholesome salad mix. The mixture
of grains is rich in B-vitamins, minerals, and fibre.

INGREDIENTS

150g (5¹/₂oz) brown rice
125g (4¹/₂oz) bulgur wheat
125g (4¹/₂oz) couscous
4 tomatoes, diced
¹/₂ cucumber, peeled and diced
50g (1³/₄oz) fresh mint, finely
    chopped
50g (1³/₄oz) fresh parsley,
    finely chopped
30g (1oz) raisins
salt and freshly ground
    black pepper

SERVES 6   **PREP** 5 MINS   **COOK** 35 MINS

1 Cook the rice in a pan of salted water for about 35 minutes until tender, or follow the instructions on the packet. Drain and set aside to cool.

2 Tip the bulgur wheat into a bowl and pour boiling water over it until it is just covered. Leave to stand for 5 minutes while you prepare the couscous in another bowl in the same way; leave this also for 5 minutes. Fluff up both the grains with a fork and then mix them together with the rice.

3 Stir the tomatoes, cucumber, herbs, and raisins into the grain mixture. Taste and then season if needed.

Nutrition data per serving

Energy	381kcals/1385kJ
Carbohydrate	73g
of which sugar	6g
Fat	2g
of which saturates	0.5g
Salt	trace
Fibre	2g

Hot and sour noodle salad with tofu

An easy, oriental-style salad. Tofu, which is made from soya beans,
is a good source of protein and calcium.

INGREDIENTS

2 tbsp sunflower oil

200g (7oz) firm tofu, cut into
  1cm x 3cm (½in x 1¼in) cubes

1 tbsp soy sauce

250g (9oz) medium rice noodles

2 red peppers, deseeded and cut
  into strips

1 white cabbage, shredded

1 red chilli, deseeded and cut
  into strips

2 tbsp fresh coriander leaves,
  roughly chopped

3 spring onions, trimmed and
  finely chopped

For the dressing

3 tbsp rice vinegar

1 tbsp soy sauce

2.5cm (1in) piece of fresh ginger,
  finely chopped

juice of 1 lime

salt and freshly ground
  black pepper

SERVES 4 **PREP 25 MINS** **COOK 20 MINS**

1 First, make the dressing. Put all the ingredients in a small bowl and whisk together. Season with a little salt and black pepper to taste. Set aside.

2 Put 1 tablespoon of the oil in a wok and, when hot, add half of the tofu and half of the soy sauce (it is easiest to cook the tofu in batches). Stir-fry for 5–10 minutes (depending on the type of tofu being used) until golden all over. Remove and set aside. Add the remaining 1 tablespoon of oil and fry the rest of the tofu, with the other half of the soy sauce, in the same way. Set aside on a plate covered with kitchen paper.

3 Put the rice noodles in a large bowl and cover with boiling water. Leave for a few minutes, or according to the instructions on the packet, until soft. Drain well.

4 Put the peppers, cabbage, and chilli in a large, shallow serving dish. Top with the drained noodles, and then add the dressing and toss to coat. Arrange the tofu on top and sprinkle with the coriander and spring onions.

Nutrition data per serving

Energy	381kcals/1590kJ
Carbohydrate	63g
of which sugar	10g
Fat	9g
of which saturates	1g
Salt	1.4g
Fibre	3g

Spicy Asian chicken salad

This colourful, summery salad is as
tasty as it is healthy.

INGREDIENTS

400g (14oz) skinless boneless
   chicken breasts

salt

1 Little Gem lettuce, shredded

100g (3½oz) beansprouts

1 large carrot, shaved using a
   vegetable peeler

15cm (6in) piece of cucumber,
   deseeded and finely sliced

½ red pepper, finely sliced

½ yellow pepper, finely sliced

approx. 15 cherry tomatoes,
   halved

small handful of mint leaves,
   chopped

small handful of coriander
   leaves, chopped

50g (1¾oz) salted peanuts,
   chopped (optional)

For the dressing

4 tbsp lime juice (approx. 2 limes)

4 tsp Thai fish sauce

1 tbsp caster sugar

pinch of chilli flakes (optional)

SERVES 4-6   **PREP** 25-30 MINS   **COOK** 15 MINS

1 Poach the chicken in a large saucepan in plenty of simmering salted
water or chicken stock for 7–10 minutes, depending on thickness,
until cooked through. Let cool, then thinly slice.

2 Whisk the dressing ingredients together, until the sugar
dissolves completely.

3 Mix together the salad vegetables, most of the herbs, and the
chicken. Mix in the dressing and scatter with the remaining herbs
and the peanuts (if using), to serve.

Nutrition data per serving

Energy	245kcals/1031kJ
Carbohydrate	13g
of which sugar	12g
Fat	8g
of which saturates	1.5g
Salt	1.3g
Fibre	4.5g

Thai beef salad

The bright, vibrant flavours of this salad really sing out,
making it perfect for a summer lunch.

INGREDIENTS

400g (14oz) thin-cut skirt
  or sirloin steak
1 tbsp sesame oil or sunflower oil
salt and freshly ground
  black pepper
2 Little Gem lettuces, leaves
  separated
large handful of watercress
20cm (8in) piece of cucumber,
  deseeded and finely sliced on
  the diagonal
1 small red onion, finely sliced
handful of coriander leaves,
  roughly chopped
handful of mint leaves,
  roughly chopped
1 red chilli, deseeded and finely
  chopped (optional)

For the dressing
4 tbsp lime juice
2 tbsp fish sauce
2 tsp soft light brown sugar
pinch of chilli flakes (optional)

SERVES 4　　　**PREP** 10 MINS　　　**COOK** 10 MINS

1 Heat a frying pan or chargrill pan. Rub the steak in the oil and season it well all over. Briefly sear on both sides so it is browned outside but still tender and juicy within. Set aside.

2 Whisk the dressing ingredients together until the sugar dissolves completely.

3 In a large bowl, mix the lettuce, watercress, cucumber, onion, herbs, and chilli (if using). Slice the still-warm steak and add to the bowl with the dressing. Toss gently, then serve.

Nutrition data per serving	
Energy	190kcals/796kJ
Carbohydrate	5.5g
of which sugar	5g
Fat	7.5g
of which saturates	2.5g
Salt	1.6g
Fibre	1g

Quinoa tabbouleh

In this healthy salad, the quinoa has a creamy, nutty taste
with a slight crunch once it is cooked.

INGREDIENTS

200g (7oz) quinoa

1/2 tsp salt

juice of 1 large lemon

125ml (9fl oz) olive oil

1 large cucumber, peeled,
   deseeded and chopped

1 large red onion, chopped

45g (1½oz) chopped parsley

45g (1½oz) chopped mint

115g (4oz) reduced-fat feta
   cheese, crumbled

100g (3½oz) Kalamata
   olives, pitted

salt and freshly ground
   black pepper

SERVES 4   **PREP 10 MINS**   **COOK 20 MINS**

1 Rinse the quinoa thoroughly in a fine mesh strainer. Drain and place it in a heavy pan. Heat, stirring constantly until the grains separate and begin to brown.

2 Add 600ml (1 pint) water and the salt and bring to the boil, stirring. Reduce the heat and cook for 15 minutes, or until the liquid is absorbed. Transfer to a bowl and set aside to cool.

3 Whisk together the lemon juice and 1 tbsp of the oil in a small bowl. Set aside.

4 Place the remaining oil, cucumber, onion, parsley, and mint in a separate, larger bowl. Add the quinoa and the lemon and oil dressing and toss. Sprinkle with the feta cheese and olives. Season to taste with salt and pepper.

Nutrition data per serving

Energy	260kcals/1096kJ
Carbohydrate	32g
of which sugar	6g
Fat	9g
of which saturates	2.5g
Salt	1.3g
Fibre	1.5g

Yellow split peas with peppers and pea shoots

Like all pulses, split peas provide good amounts of protein and dietary fibre. They are also a low-GI food. Here they are served as a tasty open sandwich.

INGREDIENTS

1 tbsp olive oil

1 small red onion, finely chopped

1 garlic clove, crushed or finely chopped

2cm (¾in) piece fresh ginger, finely chopped

85g (3oz) yellow split peas

300ml (10fl oz) vegetable stock

1 red pepper, halved

2 slices pumpernickel or toasted rye bread (about 50g/1¾oz per slice)

25g (scant 1oz) pea shoots (if unavailable, use rocket or watercress)

SERVES 2   **PREP** 15 MINS   **COOK** 35 MINS

1 Heat the oil in a small saucepan and then scatter in the onion, garlic, and ginger. Cook, stirring, for 1–2 minutes. Add the split peas and stock, bring to the boil, then cover and reduce the heat. Simmer for 30–35 minutes or until the split peas are very soft. Add a little more stock or water if needed.

2 While the split peas are cooking, prepare the red pepper: place the two halves, skin-side up, under a hot grill for 15–20 minutes or until the skin is charred and black. Cover with a clean, damp tea towel – or place in a plastic freezer bag – and allow to cool for 10 minutes. Remove the skin and seeds from the pepper. Blot the pepper dry with kitchen paper, then slice it into thick strips.

3 Place the pumpernickel bread on serving plates, spoon the split peas over it, top with the strips of red pepper, and finish with the pea shoots.

Cook's tip: Pea shoots are the leaves of the garden pea plant, and are high in vitamin C. They make an interesting alternative to traditional salad leaves – look out for them in the supermarket.

Nutrition data per serving	
Energy	348kcals/1472kJ
Carbohydrate	53g
of which sugar	5g
Fat	9g
of which saturates	1.5g
Salt	1.5g
Fibre	6g

Spiced bulgur wheat with feta and a fruity salsa

A tasty grain mixed with salty feta and fresh beans.

INGREDIENTS

280g (10oz) bulgur wheat
300ml (10fl oz) hot
    vegetable stock
150g (5½oz) fine green
    beans, chopped into
    1cm (½in) pieces
salt and freshly ground
    black pepper
125g (4½oz) reduced fat feta
    cheese, crumbled

For the salsa

½ fresh pineapple, diced
1 mango, diced
juice of ½–1 lime
1 red chilli, deseeded and
    finely chopped

SERVES 4   **PREP** 15 MINS   **COOK** 10 MINS

1 First, make the salsa: mix all the ingredients together in a small bowl and leave to sit for a while to allow the flavours to develop.

2 Tip the bulgur wheat into a large heatproof bowl and pour over the stock; it should just cover it – if not, add a little extra hot water. Allow to sit for 8–10 minutes then fluff up with a fork, separating the grains.

3 Add the beans to a pan of salted boiling water and cook for 3–5 minutes until they just soften but still have a bite to them. Drain and stir into the bulgur wheat. Season well with salt and pepper, then stir in the feta. Add a spoonful of the fruity salsa on the side and serve. You can enjoy this on its own, with a few salad leaves, or for a more substantial meal you could add a piece of grilled chicken.

Cook's tip: Bulgur wheat needs lot of flavour added to it, otherwise it can be bland, so make sure you use a well-flavoured stock.

Nutrition data per serving

Energy	370kcals/1547kJ
Carbohydrate	70g
of which sugar	16g
Fat	4g
of which saturates	2g
Salt	0.5g
Fibre	2.5g

Shredded pork and spring onion wrap

Succulent shredded pork with a Cajun-style coating.

INGREDIENTS

350g (12oz) pork tenderloin, trimmed of fat and sinew

2 bunches spring onions, sliced lengthways

4–8 Turkish flatbreads

For the marinade

1 medium onion, peeled and quartered

1 tsp freshly ground black pepper

1/2 tsp salt

1 scotch bonnet chilli, deseeded

1 tsp allspice

1/2 tsp paprika

2 ripe peaches, stoned and quartered

2 garlic cloves, peeled and roughly chopped

SERVES 4 **PREP** 10 MINS **COOK** 2 HRS

1 Preheat the oven to 150°C (300°F/Gas 2). Put the marinade ingredients into a blender and whiz to a smooth paste. Deeply slash the pork and liberally rub all over with the marinade. Place the pork in a roasting tin and cover with any remaining marinade. Cover loosely with foil and roast for 2 hours, basting occasionally.

2 Shred the pork using two forks and toss in any remaining cooking juices. Arrange on flatbreads, each with a liberal handful of spring onions, roll or fold, and serve.

Nutrition data per serving

Energy	388kcals/1440kJ
Carbohydrate	50g
of which sugar	11g
Fat	6g
of which saturates	2g
Salt	1.5g
Fibre	4g

Prawn, sweet chilli, and Greek yogurt wraps

Sweet, fresh-tasting pea shoots, juicy prawns, and sharp yogurt make a wonderful combination.

INGREDIENTS

4 large wraps

50g (1³/₄oz) pea shoots, mixed baby salad leaves, or rocket

½ cucumber, halved, deseeded, and finely sliced

175g packet of cooked, shelled king prawns, sliced in half horizontally, and deveined

3 heaped tbsp Greek yogurt

4 tsp Thai sweet chilli sauce

salt and freshly ground black pepper

SERVES 4   **PREP 10 MINS**

1 Lay the wraps on a work surface and divide the pea shoots between them, starting at the edge nearest you and covering about one-third of the wrap. Layer one-quarter of the cucumber, then the prawns, along the pea shoots, and top each with ½ tbsp of yogurt and 1 tsp of chilli sauce. Season.

2 Take the remaining yogurt and smear a little, with the back of a spoon, all over the piece of each wrap furthest from you (it should cover one-third of the wrap). This helps stick it together.

3 Fold the side nearest to you over the filling. Roll it away from you until it sticks together with the yogurt. Slice each end off and halve on a diagonal to serve.

Nutrition data per serving

Energy	249kcals/1054kJ
Carbohydrate	43g
of which sugar	5g
Fat	2g
of which saturates	1g
Salt	1.2g
Fibre	3g

Potato, pancetta, and red onion hash

Cold, leftover boiled potatoes can be chopped up
to turn this hash into a quick brunch or lunch dish.

INGREDIENTS

salt and freshly ground
    black pepper
1kg (2¼lb) floury potatoes,
    such as King Edward or
    Maris Piper, peeled and cut
    into bite-sized chunks
1 tbsp olive oil
2 red onions, finely chopped
100g (3½oz) pancetta lardons
2 tbsp finely chopped chives
baked beans and tomato
    ketchup, to serve

SERVES 4   **PREP 10 MINS**   **COOK 25 MINS**

1 Bring a saucepan of salted water to the boil, add the potatoes,
and cook for 10 minutes. Drain.

2 Meanwhile, heat the oil in a large, non-stick frying pan over a
medium heat and cook the onions for 5 minutes. Add the pancetta,
season well, and cook for a further 5 minutes, stirring occasionally.

3 Add the cooked potatoes to the frying pan and cook over a high
heat for about 15 minutes, stirring frequently.

4 Divide the hash between warmed plates and sprinkle with the
chives. Serve with baked beans and a dollop of ketchup.

Nutrition data per serving	
Energy	300kcals/1263kJ
Carbohydrate	44g
of which sugar	4g
Fat	9g
of which saturates	2.5g
Salt	0.8g
Fibre	5g

Poached eggs with chargrilled asparagus

A fabulous starter or light lunch. Dip the asparagus in the egg yolk as if it were a toast soldier.

INGREDIENTS

1 bunch of asparagus, woody ends removed
1 tbsp olive oil
salt and freshly ground black pepper
4 eggs

SERVES 4   **PREP** 5 MINS   **COOK** 10 MINS

1 Heat a chargrill pan and rub the asparagus spears with the oil. Cook on the chargrill pan over a medium heat for 5–7 minutes (depending on thickness), turning occasionally, until they are tender and charred in places. Sprinkle them with salt and pepper.

2 When the asparagus is nearly ready, bring a large pan of salted water to the boil. Crack an egg into a teacup and gently slide into the bubbling water. Repeat for all the eggs (using a teacup helps them maintain their shape). Poach the eggs in very gently simmering water for about 3 minutes until the white is set but the yolk is still runny. (The trick to perfect poached eggs is that they must be very fresh; this helps the white to stay together in a neat shape.)

3 Transfer the asparagus to warmed plates, place an egg on top of each pile, and sprinkle with black pepper.

Nutrition data per serving

Energy	128kcals/530kJ
Carbohydrate	1g
of which sugar	1g
Fat	10g
of which saturates	2g
Salt	0.2g
Fibre	1.5g

Stuffed baked potatoes

Turn a baked potato into a complete, balanced meal
with this simple, tasty stuffing.

INGREDIENTS

4 baking potatoes

25g (scant 1oz) butter,
softened

salt and freshly ground
black pepper

2 tomatoes, deseeded
and finely chopped

100g (3½oz) ham, finely
chopped

2 spring onions, finely
chopped (optional)

100g (3½oz) grated cheese,
such as Cheddar

green salad, to serve

MAKES 8   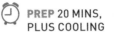 **PREP** 20 MINS,
PLUS COOLING   **COOK** 1 HR 20 MINS

1 Preheat the oven to 200°C (400°F/Gas 6). Prick each potato and
bake on an oven shelf for 1 hour. Leave to cool. Cut each in half
lengthways and use a spoon to scoop out the middles. Put the scooped-
out potato in a bowl and mash with the butter and seasoning.

2 Mix the tomato into the mash potato with the ham, spring onions
(if using), and half the cheese.

3 Stuff back inside the skins. Place on a baking tray and scatter with
the remaining cheese.

4 Bake for 20 minutes, until brown, crispy, and hot through. Cool for
5 minutes before serving with a green salad.

Nutrition data per serving

Energy	187kcals/786kJ
Carbohydrate	21g
of which sugar	2g
Fat	8g
of which saturates	4.5g
Salt	0.7g
Fibre	2.5g

Sweet potatoes with a smoky tomato filling

A tasty and filling light lunch, which is low in fat and salt.

INGREDIENTS

4 sweet potatoes, unpeeled
2 tbsp olive oil
1 small red onion, finely chopped
1 small red pepper, deseeded and diced
1/2 red chilli, deseeded and finely chopped
225g (8oz) cherry tomatoes, halved
150g (5oz) sweetcorn, defrosted if frozen
1/2 tsp smoked sweet paprika
salt and freshly ground black pepper

SERVES 2   **PREP** 5 MINS   **COOK** 40 MINS

1 Preheat the oven to 180°C (350°F/Gas 4). Pierce the sweet potatoes in several places and put in the oven for 40 minutes or until cooked.

2 Meanwhile, heat the oil in a frying pan, add the onion and cook for 1–2 minutes. Stir in the red pepper and chilli; cook for a further 1–2 minutes or until the pepper is starting to soften. Add the cherry tomatoes, sweetcorn, and paprika. Season to taste with salt and black pepper, and cook for a further 1–2 minutes.

3 Slice the potatoes in half and spoon the tomato mixture over them.

Nutrition data per serving

Energy	289kcals/1226kJ
Carbohydrate	55g
of which sugar	17g
Fat	7g
of which saturates	1g
Salt	0.2g
Fibre	7g

Mixed bean burger

Vegetarian burgers with a hint of Indian spice.

INGREDIENTS

1 red onion, roughly chopped

2 garlic cloves, finely chopped

1 green chilli, deseeded and
   roughly chopped

pinch of garam masala

handful of fresh coriander

2 x 400g cans of mixed beans,
   drained

125g (4½oz) mushrooms, grated

salt and freshly ground
   black pepper

2 tbsp fresh breadcrumbs

1–2 eggs, lightly beaten

2 tbsp sunflower oil

SERVES 4–8   **PREP** 10 MINS, PLUS CHILLING   **COOK** 15 MINS

1 Place the onion, garlic, chilli, garam masala, coriander, beans, and mushrooms in a food processor and whiz until well combined, but do not overblend and let it become mushy.

2 Season well with salt and black pepper then tip in the breadcrumbs and a little of the egg and pulse until it all binds together but is neither too wet nor too dry – add a little more egg if needed. Shape into 8 patties, arrange on a plate and transfer to the refrigerator for 20 minutes to firm up.

3 Heat the oil in a non-stick frying pan and cook a few burgers at a time for 6–7 minutes or until the underside starts to brown. Turn over the burgers using a fish slice and cook the other side for the same amount of time, adding more oil if needed. You could serve these in wholemeal bread rolls, each with a small quantity of tomato salad.

Nutrition data per serving

Energy	250kcals/1061kJ
Carbohydrate	37g
of which sugar	4g
Fat	5g
of which saturates	1g
Salt	0.3g
Fibre	12g

Red lentil dhal with cherry tomatoes

A quick and tasty lunch or supper. Unlike other pulses,
lentils don't need to be soaked before cooking.

INGREDIENTS

2 tbsp vegetable oil

1 large onion, peeled and
finely chopped

3 garlic cloves, peeled and
crushed or finely chopped

5mm (¼in) piece of fresh ginger,
peeled and finely chopped

200g (7oz) red lentils, rinsed

1 red chilli, deseeded and
finely chopped

½ tsp salt

freshly ground black pepper

200g (7oz) cherry
tomatoes, halved

1 tsp black mustard
seeds (optional)

3 tbsp chopped fresh coriander

SERVES 4   **PREP 10 MINS**   **COOK 40 MINS**

1 Heat the oil in a large saucepan, add the onion and cook over a low heat, stirring occasionally, for 5 minutes. Add the garlic and ginger and continue to cook for 1–2 minutes.

2 Add the lentils, chilli, salt, and 750ml (1¼ pints) water. Bring to the boil, reduce the heat, and simmer for 30 minutes or until the lentils are soft. Season to taste with freshly ground black pepper.

3 Stir in the tomatoes, mustard seeds if using, and coriander. Serve with chapattis and raita.

Nutrition data per serving

Energy	231kcals/965kJ
Carbohydrate	33g
of which sugar	4.5g
Fat	7g
of which saturates	1g
Salt	0.1g
Fibre	3.5g

Catalan seafood zarzuela

This traditional Catalan stew makes an opulent starter or summer lunch. Add more mussels if you can't find clams.

INGREDIENTS

1 tbsp olive oil
1 onion, finely chopped
2 garlic cloves, finely chopped
300ml (10fl oz) dry white wine
300ml (10fl oz) fish stock
2 tbsp tomato purée
generous pinch of saffron threads
salt and freshly ground
    black pepper
12 live mussels, scrubbed, and
    beards removed (discard
    any that stay open when
    sharply tapped)
12 live clams, scrubbed (discard
    any that stay open when
    sharply tapped)
300g (10oz) firm white fish fillets,
    such as haddock or cod,
    pin-boned, skinned, and
    cut into bite-sized pieces
2 squid pouches (approx.
    175g/6oz in total), sliced
    into 5mm- (¼in-) thick rings
8 raw king prawns,
    shells on, deveined
3 tbsp chopped flat-leaf
    parsley leaves
crusty bread, to serve

SERVES 4   **PREP 15 MINS**   **COOK 25 MINS**

1 Heat the oil in a deep-sided sauté pan over a medium heat and fry the onion for 10 minutes, covered. Add the garlic and cook for 1 minute. Add the wine and simmer for 5 minutes. Add the stock, tomato purée, and saffron, and season. Return to a simmer, add the mussels and clams. Cook for 3 minutes.

2 Add the white fish, squid, and prawns, and cook for 2 minutes. Cover and cook for 5 minutes more. Discard any mussels or clams that do not open on cooking. Stir in the parsley. Serve with crusty bread.

Nutrition data per serving

Energy	314kcals/1319kJ
Carbohydrate	7g
of which sugar	3g
Fat	6g
of which saturates	1g
Salt	2.3g
Fibre	0.5g

Mini pizzas

These individual pizzas are perfect to make with children,
and can be topped and cooked at the last minute.

INGREDIENTS

For the bases

250g (9oz) strong bread flour,
  plus extra for dusting

1/4 tsp salt

1 1/2 tsp dried yeast

1 tbsp olive oil, plus extra for
  greasing

For the topping

400g can crushed tomatoes,
  or 400ml (14fl oz) passata

2 garlic cloves, crushed

1 tbsp olive oil

freshly ground black pepper

selection of prepared pizza
  toppings

150g (5 1/2 oz) finely sliced
  mozzarella

MAKES 10   **PREP** 20 MINS,
                 PLUS RISING   **COOK** 10 MINS

1 Put the flour and salt into a large bowl, or the bowl of a food processor fitted with a dough hook. Dissolve the yeast in 175ml (6fl oz) of warm water, then add the oil.

2 If making by hand, make a well in the centre of the flour. Gradually pour in the liquid, stirring to form a rough dough. Use your hands to bring it together. Turn the dough out onto a floured work surface. Knead for up to 10 minutes, until smooth, glossy, and elastic.

3 If making in a food processor, turn the machine on to a low speed. Pour in the liquid a little at a time, until the mixture begins to come together. You may need to turn off the machine and scrape down the sides once or twice to ensure that all the flour is incorporated. Increase the speed to medium and continue to knead for 5–7 minutes, until smooth, glossy, and elastic.

4 Put the dough in an oiled bowl and cover loosely with cling film. Leave to rise in a warm place for 2 hours, or until doubled in size.

5 Meanwhile, make the tomato sauce. Put the tomatoes, garlic, and olive oil into a small saucepan, and season well with pepper. Bring to the boil, reduce the heat to a low simmer, and cook for 45 minutes to 1 hour, until you have a rich, thick sauce. Adjust the seasoning.

6 When ready to cook, preheat the oven to 230°C (450°F/Gas 8). When the dough has risen, turn it out onto a lightly floured work surface and knead it briefly. Divide it into 10 equal-sized pieces, and roll each one out to a diameter of 12–15cm (5–6in). Lay them on several baking sheets.

7 Top the mini pizzas with 1 tbsp of the tomato sauce, spread thinly, and any toppings you would like. Finish with a thin layer of mozzarella cheese, and cook at the top of the hot oven for 10 minutes, until golden brown and crispy.

Nutrition data per serving	
Energy	151kcals/673kJ
Carbohydrate	19g
of which sugar	1.5g
Fat	5.5g
of which saturates	2.5g
Salt	0.4g
Fibre	1.5g

Lemon, garlic and parsley linguine

An instant meal when there is little in the fridge: you just need fresh parsley, garlic, olive oil, and lemon to transform pasta into something special.

INGREDIENTS

350g (12oz) linguine
3 tbsp olive oil
2 garlic cloves, finely chopped
juice of 1 lemon and zest
    of ½ lemon
handful of fresh flat-leaf parsley,
    finely chopped
pinch of chilli flakes (optional)
salt and freshly ground
    black pepper

SERVES 4   **PREP 5 MINS**   **COOK 10 MINS**

1 Add the linguine to a large pan of salted boiling water and cook for 8–10 minutes or according to the instructions on the packet. Drain, then return to the pan with a little of the cooking water and toss together.

2 While the pasta is cooking, heat the oil in a frying pan, add the garlic and cook on a very low heat, being very careful not to burn the garlic. Cook for about 1 minute, then add the lemon zest and juice and cook for a couple more minutes.

3 Stir in the parsley and chilli flakes, if using. Season with salt and black pepper and then add the mixture to the pasta and toss to coat. A tomato and basil salad would work well with this dish.

Nutrition data per serving

Energy	350kcals/1477kJ
Carbohydrate	65g
of which sugar	3g
Fat	7g
of which saturates	1g
Salt	trace
Fibre	2.5g

Spicy udon noodles with tuna

Thick juicy noodles tossed with hot and sweet fresh tuna.

INGREDIENTS

1 tsp wasabi paste

2–3 tbsp dark soy sauce

1–2 tsp runny honey

4 tuna steaks

2 tsp sunflower oil

2 garlic cloves, finely sliced

5cm (2in) piece of fresh
root ginger, finely sliced

600g (1lb 5oz) thick
udon noodles

handful of coriander leaves

lime wedges, to serve

SERVES 4 **PREP 15 MINS, PLUS MARINATING** **COOK 15 MINS**

1 First make the marinade: mix together the wasabi paste, 2 tablespoons of soy sauce, and the honey in a bowl. Add the tuna, turning each steak to coat, and leave to marinate for 15 minutes. Heat a griddle pan, add the tuna steaks (reserving the marinade) two at a time, and cook undisturbed for 2–3 minutes. Turn the steaks over using tongs (they should lift quite easily) and cook on the other side for the same time. The steaks should still be a little pink inside. Remove from the heat and set aside.

2 Heat the sunflower oil in a wok, add the garlic and ginger and keep stirring to prevent burning. Pour in the reserved marinade and allow it to bubble, then add the noodles and stir for a couple of minutes until softened.

3 Slice the tuna into strips, add to the wok, and mix together with the other ingredients. Season with a little extra soy sauce if desired, sprinkle over the coriander, and serve with lime wedges.

Cook's tip: Wasabi is Japanese horseradish and is very hot, so use sparingly. You can buy it as powder and add water instead of as a ready-made paste, but be warned that this makes a hotter wasabi.

Nutrition data per serving

Energy	443kcals/181kJ
Carbohydrate	45g
of which sugar	1g
Fat	10g
of which saturates	2g
Salt	1.5g
Fibre	2g

DINNER

Keralan fish curry

The flavour and aroma of this exotic curry is beautifully subtle
and fragrant, so try it with any firm white fish.

INGREDIENTS

800g (1¾lb) skinless haddock
   fillets, cut into bite-sized pieces

2 tsp ground turmeric

salt and freshly ground
   black pepper

1 tbsp vegetable oil

1 large onion, finely sliced

1 tsp black mustard seeds

5 curry leaves

4cm (1½in) fresh root ginger,
   finely chopped

2 tbsp tamarind paste

200ml (7fl oz) coconut milk

150ml (5fl oz) fish stock

2 spring onions, finely sliced

1 red chilli, deseeded and finely
   chopped (optional)

basmati rice and chopped
   coriander leaves, to serve

SERVES 4   **PREP** 10 MINS   **COOK** 15 MINS

1 Place the haddock in a bowl, sprinkle with the turmeric, season, and
stir to coat. Set aside.

2 Heat the oil in a large, non-stick frying pan over a medium heat, and
add the onion, black mustard seeds, and curry leaves. Fry gently for
10 minutes, stirring occasionally, until the onion is lightly brown.

3 Add the ginger and cook for 1 or 2 minutes, then add the tamarind
paste, coconut milk, and stock, and stir well. Heat the sauce to a
gentle simmer.

4 Add the fish and simmer gently for 3–4 minutes or until it is just
cooked. Stir in the spring onions and chilli (if using).

5 Serve the curry with basmati rice, sprinkled with chopped
coriander leaves.

Nutrition data per serving

Energy	213kcals/905kJ
Carbohydrate	5.5g
of which sugar	5g
Fat	4.5g
of which saturates	0.5g
Salt	0.8g
Fibre	0.8g

Haddock and spinach gratin

A hearty and healthy fish pie topped with golden wholemeal breadcrumbs.

INGREDIENTS

3 slices wholemeal bread, torn

350g (12oz) skinless and
  boneless haddock

600ml (1 pint) semi-skimmed milk

salt and freshly ground
  black pepper

25g (scant 1oz)
  polyunsaturated margarine

1 tbsp flour

pinch of paprika

150g (5½oz) young spinach
  leaves, roughly torn

3 spring onion stalks,
  finely chopped

25g (scant 1oz) Parmesan
  cheese, grated

pinch of chilli flakes

SERVES 4   **PREP** 15-20 MINS   **COOK** 20 MINS

1 Preheat the oven to 200°C (400°F/Gas 6). Put the bread in a food processor or blender and whizz to make breadcrumbs. Tip these into a shallow tin and cook in the oven for 5–8 minutes until beginning to turn golden. Remove from the oven and tip back into the food processor.

2 Put the fish in a pan and cover with the milk. Season well. Simmer gently over a low heat for 5 minutes, or until the fish breaks up when poked. Remove with a slotted spoon and put on a plate. Pour the milk into a jug.

3 Melt the margarine in the pan, remove it from the heat and stir in the flour and a little of the reserved cooking milk. Return the pan to the heat and gradually add the remainder of the milk, stirring continually. Cook, stirring, until it thickens into a smooth sauce. Stir in the paprika and season really well with lots of black pepper.

4 Stir the spinach into the sauce (you could precook the spinach for a couple of minutes if you wish) along with the spring onions. Mix the sauce with the fish, taking care not to break up the fish. Spoon the mixture into an ovenproof dish or individual dishes.

5 Add the Parmesan cheese and chilli flakes to the breadcrumbs in the food processor. Whizz again until a fine blend, then scatter evenly over the fish mixture. Cook in the oven for 10–15 minutes until bubbling around the edges; the top should be golden.

Nutrition data per serving

Energy	335kcals/1411kJ
Carbohydrate	25g
of which sugar	8g
Fat	13.5g
of which saturates	5g
Salt	1.2g
Fibre	3g

Spiced noodles with aromatic red snapper

Sambal oelek, an Indonesian hot chilli condiment,
is the perfect partner for this delicate fish.

INGREDIENTS

1 red snapper, filleted, skinned, and
chopped into large chunks

250g (9oz) dried fine rice noodles

1 tbsp sunflower oil

bunch of spring onions, sliced

300g (10oz) French beans, trimmed
and chopped

1 red pepper, deseeded and
finely chopped

2 garlic cloves, finely chopped

1–2 tsp sambal oelek, or 1 chopped
red chilli, or ½–1 tsp dried
chilli flakes mixed with 1 tsp
vegetable oil

1 tbsp tamari or soy sauce

handful of fresh coriander, leaves only

1 orange, peeled and segmented

For the marinade

zest and juice of 1 orange

2 tsp finely chopped thyme leaves

1 red chilli, deseeded and
finely chopped

2 garlic cloves, finely chopped

1 tbsp olive oil

salt and freshly ground black pepper

SERVES 4   ⏰ **PREP** 15 MINS, PLUS MARINATING   **COOK** 25-30 MINS

1 Place the fish in a shallow dish. Combine all the marinade ingredients in a jug, stir well, and pour over the fish, turning the pieces to coat. Set aside to marinate for up to 1 hour. Preheat the oven to 180°C (350°F/Gas 4). Remove the fish using a slotted spoon and place in a roasting tin. Roast for 20–25 minutes or until the fish is cooked through and turning opaque. Set aside.

2 Cover the noodles with boiling water and leave for 10 minutes or as per pack instructions. Drain. Add the oil to the wok or pan and swirl it around. Add the spring onions and cook on a medium-high heat for 2–3 minutes until soft. Add the beans and stir. Cook for about 5 minutes until they begin to soften. Stir in the pepper and garlic and cook for 2–3 minutes.

3 Add the sambal oelek and tamari. Add the noodles and toss. Cook for 3–5 minutes and transfer to a serving dish. Top with the fish and coriander. Serve with the orange segments.

Nutrition data per serving	
Energy	473kcals/1982kJ
Carbohydrate	59g
of which sugar	11g
Fat	8g
of which saturates	1g
Salt	1g
Fibre	4g

Minted pea and prawn risotto

Sweet peas and prawns contrast well with the sharp Parmesan and creamy rice.

INGREDIENTS

400g (14oz) frozen peas

salt and freshly ground
black pepper

750ml (1¼ pints) fish
or vegetable stock

1 tbsp olive oil

1 onion, finely chopped

1 garlic clove, finely chopped

300g (10oz) risotto rice, such as
Arborio or Carnaroli

120ml (4fl oz) white wine (optional)

300g (10oz) cooked, shelled, and
deveined large prawns

30g (1oz) finely grated Parmesan
cheese, plus extra to serve

2 tbsp chopped mint leaves

1 tbsp butter (optional)

SERVES 4   **PREP 10 MINS**   **COOK 25 MINS**

1 Cook the peas in boiling salted water for 2 minutes, until just cooked. Drain, refresh under cold water, then purée with about 200ml (7fl oz) of the stock in a food processor, or with a hand-held blender, until smooth. Put the remaining stock in a saucepan over a low heat, and keep it simmering on the stove, with a ladle nearby.

2 Heat the oil in a large, heavy-based, deep-sided frying pan. Cook the onion over a medium heat for 5 minutes, until it softens, but does not brown. Add the garlic and cook for a further minute.

3 Tip in the rice and stir to coat. When it sizzles, stir in the wine (if using) and allow it to evaporate.

4 Add the stock a ladleful at a time, stirring constantly, for 20 minutes, allowing the liquid to evaporate between ladlefuls.

5 Add the puréed peas and cook for 2 minutes, or until most of the liquid evaporates. The rice should be al dente. Add the prawns and a further ladle of stock, and heat through for 2 minutes.

6 Take the pan off the heat and add the Parmesan, mint, and butter (if using), and season well to taste. Sprinkle with extra Parmesan to serve.

Nutrition data per serving	
Energy	542kcals/2262kJ
Carbohydrate	68g
of which sugar	4g
Fat	11g
of which saturates	4.5g
Salt	1.9g
Fibre	7g

Quick paella

Frozen foods can often help you out when time is short, and frozen seafood adds flavour and body to this dish.

INGREDIENTS

1 tbsp olive oil

200g (7oz) skinless boneless chicken breast, cut into strips

400g (14oz) frozen seafood mix, defrosted and drained

1 Spanish onion, sliced

2 garlic cloves, finely chopped

1 tsp turmeric

1 tsp smoked paprika

salt and freshly ground black pepper

300g (10oz) easy-cook long-grain white rice

1 litre (1¾ pints) hot chicken stock

100g (3½oz) frozen green beans

100g (3½oz) frozen peas

juice of ½ lemon

SERVES 4   **PREP** 10 MINS   **COOK** 35–40 MINS

1 Heat half the oil in a very large, non-stick frying pan, with a lid, over a medium heat. Add the chicken and cook for 5 minutes, stirring occasionally. Remove from the pan and set aside.

2 Add the seafood mix to the pan and cook for 2 minutes, stirring occasionally. Remove from the pan using a slotted spoon and set aside with the chicken.

3 Wipe the pan dry with kitchen paper and add the remaining ½ tbsp of oil. Add the onion and cook for 5 minutes. Add the garlic and cook for 1 minute.

4 Add the spices, seasoning, and rice to the pan, and stir to coat for 1 minute. Add the stock, bring to the boil, cover, and simmer for 10–15 minutes.

5 Add the beans to the pan, stir well, and cook for a further 3 minutes, then add the peas and cook for 2 minutes.

6 Return the cooked chicken and seafood to the pan and heat through over a high heat for a final 2 minutes, stirring constantly. Squeeze the lemon over and serve immediately.

Nutrition data per serving

Energy	522kcals/2188kJ
Carbohydrate	62g
of which sugar	2.5g
Fat	6g
of which saturates	1g
Salt	1.3g
Fibre	3g

Linguine with spicy prawn and tomato sauce

Adding Parmesan cheese is not traditional with shellfish pasta recipes, but feel free to have some if you want!

INGREDIENTS

400g (14oz) shell-on, cooked prawns
2 tbsp olive oil
1 onion, finely chopped
2 garlic cloves, crushed
1 tsp chilli flakes
400g can chopped tomatoes
1 tbsp tomato purée
1 tsp caster sugar
2 tbsp roughly chopped flat-leaf parsley leaves
salt and freshly ground black pepper
300g (10oz) dried linguine

SERVES 4   🕐 **PREP** 20 MINS   **COOK** 1 HR

1 First, shell the prawns and devein them. Cover and refrigerate. Put the shells in a saucepan and pour in a 5cm (2in) depth of water. Bring to the boil, reduce to a low simmer, and cook for 25–30 minutes until the liquid has reduced by about half. Strain into a jug.

2 Heat the oil in a heavy-based saucepan and cook the onion over a medium heat for about 5 minutes, until softened but not browned. Add the garlic and chilli flakes and cook for 1 minute.

3 Add the tomatoes and prawn stock. Stir in the tomato purée, sugar, and parsley, and season well. Bring the sauce to the boil, reduce the heat to a low simmer, and cook for about 45 minutes until thickened and reduced. If the tomatoes are taking a while to break down, mash gently with a potato masher to help them along.

4 When the sauce is nearly ready, cook the linguine in boiling salted water according to the packet instructions. Drain (reserving a ladleful of the cooking water) and return it to the pan with the reserved water.

5 Add the prawns to the sauce and cook for 2 minutes, or until heated through, being careful not to overcook. Toss the sauce through the linguine to serve.

Nutrition data per serving

Energy	467kcals/1971kJ
Carbohydrate	59g
of which sugar	7g
Fat	11g
of which saturates	1.5g
Salt	0.2g
Fibre	4.5g

Wild rice, courgette, fennel, and prawn pan-fry

Wild rice adds a delicate, nutty flavour to this pan-fry.

INGREDIENTS

2 tbsp olive oil

1 red onion, finely chopped

3 courgettes, diced

salt and freshly ground
   black pepper

1 fennel bulb, trimmed and
   finely chopped

225g (8oz) mixed long-grain
   and wild rice.

900ml (1½ pints) vegetable stock

200g (7oz) peeled prawns, raw

2 garlic cloves, chopped

1 tbsp flat-leaf parsley,
   finely chopped

4 lemon wedges, to serve

SERVES 4   **PREP** 15 MINS   **COOK** 35 MINS

1 Heat half the oil in a large frying pan and add the onion. Cook over a low heat for 5 minutes, or until it softens. Stir in the courgettes and cook for 5 minutes, or until they begin to colour slightly. Season well with salt and black pepper.

2 Add the fennel and continue cooking over a low heat for 5 minutes, or until it softens. Stir in the mixed rice. Pour in a little of the stock and bring to the boil. Reduce the heat to a simmer, then add most of the remaining stock and cook for 20–25 minutes or until the wild rice starts to split. Add more hot stock if needed.

3 Meanwhile, heat the remaining oil in a frying pan, add the prawns, and cook for a few minutes until they turn pink. Throw in the garlic and toss with the prawns. Remove from the heat and stir in the parsley. Spoon the rice mixture into a large serving dish, and tip the prawns over it. Serve with the lemon wedges.

Cook's tip: Alternatively, you could use cooked prawns for ease; once the rice is cooked, just stir them in and warm through.

Nutrition data per serving

Energy	366kcals/1528kJ
Carbohydrate	52g
of which sugar	4g
Fat	8g
of which saturates	1.5g
Salt	1.4g
Fibre	2g

Haddock and green bean pie

Flakes of fish in a creamy tarragon sauce, topped with crispy breadcrumbs.

INGREDIENTS

2 slices of wholemeal bread

1 tbsp olive oil

1 onion, finely chopped

salt and freshly ground
　black pepper

200g (7oz) green beans,
　trimmed and halved

3 garlic cloves, finely chopped

1 tbsp white wine vinegar

1 tbsp plain flour

300ml (10fl oz) milk

few tarragon leaves,
　finely chopped

500g (1lb 2oz) haddock
　fillets, skinned

SERVES 4　　**PREP** 10 MINS　　**COOK** 30 MINS

1 Preheat the oven to 200°C (400°F/Gas 6). Put the bread in a food processor or blender and whizz until it forms breadcrumbs, then set aside.

2 Heat the olive oil in a large frying pan, add the onion and cook for about 3 minutes until soft and translucent. Season with some salt and black pepper, then add the beans and garlic and cook for a further minute. Add the vinegar, increase the heat and cook for 1 minute.

3 Remove the pan from the heat, stir in the flour to combine, add a little milk and stir again until all the flour is mixed in. Reduce the heat, return the pan to the hob and slowly pour in the rest of the milk, stirring continuously to make a smooth sauce (you can use a balloon whisk to prevent lumps forming).

4 Remove the pan from the heat and stir in the tarragon. Season to taste. Lay the fish in an ovenproof baking dish, pour the sauce over it and stir to combine. Sprinkle with the breadcrumbs and cook in the oven for about 20 minutes or until the fish is done and the breadcrumbs are golden.

Nutrition data per serving

Energy	246kcals/1037kJ
Carbohydrate	17g
of which sugar	6g
Fat	7g
of which saturates	2.5g
Salt	0.5g
Fibre	2g

Crab and tomato pasta

Pasta absorbs wonderfully the sweet flavour of crab.
This is an easy dish for last-minute entertaining.

INGREDIENTS

1 tbsp olive oil

1 onion, very finely chopped

1 celery stick, very
  finely chopped

1 bay leaf

salt and freshly ground
  black pepper

2 garlic cloves, finely chopped

1 red chilli, deseeded and
  finely chopped

100ml (3½fl oz) dry white wine

150ml (5fl oz) passata

350g (12oz) linguine or other
  pasta shapes

250g (9oz) fresh white crab meat

handful of flat-leaf parsley,
  finely chopped

SERVES 4   **PREP** 15 MINS   **COOK** 30 MINS

1 Heat the oil in a large pan, add the onion, and cook over a low heat for 5–6 minutes until soft. Add the celery, bay leaf, and salt and pepper, and cook gently on a low heat, stirring, for about 10 minutes, making sure the vegetables don't brown. Stir in the garlic and chilli, and cook for another minute.

2 Raise the heat, add the wine, and let it bubble for 1 minute. Add the passata and let this bubble for 2–3 minutes. Reduce to a low heat and simmer gently for about 15 minutes.

3 Put the pasta in a large pan of boiling salted water and cook according to instructions. Give it a stir at the beginning of cooking to prevent it from sticking together. Drain and return to the pan with a little of the cooking water. Stir the crab meat into the tomato sauce and warm through. Pour the sauce over the linguine and toss to combine. Sprinkle over the parsley and serve straight away.

Nutrition data per serving

Energy	446kcals/1888kJ
Carbohydrate	66g
of which sugar	3.5g
Fat	8g
of which saturates	1g
Salt	0.7g
Fibre	4.5g

Spiced lamb flatbread

In Turkey, this street food is served garnished with a sprinkling
of flat-leaf parsley and a squeeze of lemon.

INGREDIENTS

300g (10oz) plain flour blend,
  plus extra for dusting

1 tsp salt

1 tsp caster sugar

½ tsp baking powder

3 tbsp oil

For the topping

2 tsp ground cumin

½–1 tsp chilli powder

1 red pepper, deseeded and
  roughly chopped

1 red onion, roughly chopped

1 garlic clove

handful of flat-leaf parsley,
  plus extra to garnish

175g (6oz) lamb mince

lemon and salad, to serve

MAKES 6

**PREP 20 MINS,
PLUS RESTING**

COOK 20-25 MINS

1 Sift the flour, salt, and baking powder into a large bowl. Pour 325ml (11fl oz) lukewarm water and 2 tablespoons oil into the flour, mix to a slightly sticky, soft dough, and knead on a lightly floured surface for 5 minutes until smooth and elastic. Divide into 6 balls, place on oiled baking sheets, and cover with clean damp tea towels. Set aside in a warm place.

2 Preheat the oven to 200°C (400°F/Gas 6). For the topping, whizz together the spices, pepper, onion, garlic, and parsley in a food processor until finely chopped. Strain and discard the juice. Transfer to a bowl, add 1 tablespoon oil and the lamb mince, and season.

3 Roll out the dough balls into thin, flat ovals and place on oiled baking sheets. Spread a thin layer of the lamb mixture over each oval, leaving a thin border clear around the edges. Bake for 20–25 minutes or until the bread is crisp and the topping is cooked. Top with parsley and a squeeze of lemon, fold in half lengthways, and serve with salad for a light supper.

Nutrition data per serving	
Energy	371kcals/1565kJ
Carbohydrate	58g
of which sugar	4g
Fat	9.5g
of which saturates	2.4g
Salt	0.8g
Fibre	4g

Salt-and-pepper beef noodles

Succulent strips of beef are stir-fried in a Chinese-style
sauce with crisp mangetout.

INGREDIENTS

200g (7oz) dried rice noodles

600g (1lb 5oz) sirloin steak,
thinly sliced

salt and freshly ground
black pepper

1 tsp Sichuan pepper

1 tbsp sunflower oil

3 garlic cloves, finely sliced

5cm (2in) piece of fresh root
ginger, peeled and finely sliced

1 green chilli, deseeded and
sliced into fine strips

200g (7oz) mangetout or
sugarsnap peas, sliced (optional)

3 spring onions, finely sliced,
to garnish

For the sauce

2 tbsp tamari or soy sauce

1 tbsp nam pla (fish sauce)

1 tbsp cornflour

1 tsp caster sugar

SERVES 4   **PREP 15 MINS**   **COOK 20 MINS**

1 Place the noodles in a bowl, cover with boiling water, and leave
for 10 minutes or as per pack instructions. Drain and set aside.

2 For the sauce, mix together the tamari, nam pla, cornflour,
and sugar and set aside.

3 Toss the beef with the salt and pepper and Sichuan pepper. Heat
the oil in a wok, add the beef, and stir-fry on a medium-high heat
for 3–4 minutes or until browned all over, then remove.

4 Add the garlic, ginger, chilli, and mangetout or sugarsnap peas (if
using) to the wok, adding a little more oil if needed, and stir-fry for
2 minutes on a medium-high heat. Pour in the sauce and let it bubble.
Add 2–3 tablespoons water – more if it is still too thick – and let it cook
for 2 more minutes. Return the beef to the wok and stir to coat, then
add the noodles and stir again. Spoon out into a serving dish and top
with the spring onion.

Nutrition data per serving

Energy	450kcals/1884kJ
Carbohydrate	46g
of which sugar	4g
Fat	10g
of which saturates	3g
Salt	1.9g
Fibre	1.2g

Griddled steak chunks with herby rice

A tasty and filling dish for red meat lovers.

INGREDIENTS

2 tbsp olive oil

1 red onion, finely chopped

salt and freshly ground
 black pepper

2 garlic cloves, finely chopped

225g (8oz) basmati rice

900ml (1½ pints) vegetable stock

125g (4½oz) frozen peas

handful of flat-leaf parsley,
 finely chopped

handful of fresh mint,
 finely chopped

handful of fresh coriander,
 finely chopped

500g (1lb 2oz) lean steak

SERVES 4   **PREP** 10 MINS   **COOK** 30 MINS

1 Heat 1 tablespoon of the oil in a large frying pan and add half the onion. Cook over a low heat for 5 minutes or until soft. Season with salt and pepper, then stir in the garlic. Add the rice and stir to coat with the oil.

2 Pour in a little of the stock and let it bubble, add a little more, and stir again. Gradually add the rest of the stock as it is absorbed and cook for 15 minutes until the rice is soft and tender, then stir in the peas. Heat through for 1–2 minutes, then remove from the heat and stir in the herbs. Cover with a lid and set aside.

3 Coat the steak with the remaining olive oil and season. Heat a griddle pan until hot, then add the steak and grill for 3–5 minutes each side or until cooked to your liking. Remove and let rest for a few minutes, then slice and arrange over the rice. Sprinkle over the remaining onion and serve.

Nutrition data per serving

Energy	488kcals/2039kJ
Carbohydrate	52g
of which sugar	2.5g
Fat	13g
of which saturates	3.5g
Salt	1.3g
Fibre	2g

Venison and red wine stew

Venison is an excellent source of low-fat protein, and its treatment
in this recipe gives it a rich, satisfying flavour.

INGREDIENTS

3 tbsp olive oil

4 shallots, halved

2 celery sticks, finely chopped

1 carrot, finely chopped

2 garlic cloves, finely chopped

2 tbsp plain flour

$^1/_2$ tsp grated nutmeg

$^1/_2$ tsp ground allspice

salt and freshly ground
   black pepper

675g (1$^1/_2$lb) boneless shoulder
   or other stewing venison,
   cut into bite-sized chunks

4 tbsp redcurrant jelly

finely grated zest and juice
   of 1 orange

300ml (10fl oz) red wine

150ml (5fl oz) beef stock

1 bay leaf

potato and celeriac mash,
   to serve

SERVES 4   **PREP** 15 MINS   **COOK** 2 HRS 15 MINS
-2 HRS 45 MINS

1 Preheat the oven to 150°C (300°F/Gas 2). Heat 1 tbsp of the oil in
a medium flameproof casserole and gently fry the shallots, celery,
and carrot for 3 minutes. Add the garlic and cook for a couple more
minutes. Remove from the casserole using a slotted spoon and set aside.

2 Place the flour, nutmeg, and allspice in a large freezer bag, season
well, and add the meat. Shake to coat the meat in the seasoned
flour. Tip out into a sieve and shake to remove excess flour.

3 Add the remaining 2 tbsp of oil to the casserole and brown the meat
in batches over a medium heat, removing each batch on to the plate
with the vegetables.

4 Add the redcurrant jelly, orange zest and juice, wine, stock, and
bay leaf to the casserole, season, and stir until the jelly has melted.

5 Return the vegetables and venison, stir, and bring to a simmer.
Cover and cook in the oven for 2–2$^1/_2$ hours or until the venison is
tender. Remove the bay leaf and serve the stew with potato and celeriac
mash, made with two-thirds potato to one-third celeriac.

Nutrition data per serving	
Energy	400kcals/1670kJ
Carbohydrate	21g
of which sugar	16g
Fat	11g
of which saturates	2.5g
Salt	0.4g
Fibre	2g

Slow-cooked shoulder of pork

Also known as pulled pork, this is cooked until it falls apart juicily,
shredded, then smothered in delicious sauce.

INGREDIENTS

2 tbsp sunflower oil, plus extra
    for rubbing

1 onion, finely chopped

2 garlic cloves, crushed

100ml (3½fl oz) tomato ketchup

4 tbsp cider vinegar

1 tsp Tabasco or other hot sauce

1 tsp Worcestershire sauce

1 tsp dried mustard powder

2 tbsp runny honey

2kg (4½lb) bone-in pork shoulder

salt, for rubbing

selection of tortilla wraps, soured
    cream, salsa, guacamole,
    lettuce, and finely sliced
    red onions, to serve

SERVES 6-8   **PREP** 30 MINS,   **COOK** 3 HRS,
                        PLUS MARINATING   PLUS RESTING

1 Heat the oil in a small, heavy-based pan. Fry the onion over a
medium heat for 5 minutes until softened. Add the garlic and cook
for 1 minute. Add the remaining ingredients, apart from the pork and
salt, with 100ml (3½fl oz) of water, and whisk well.

2 Bring to the boil, reduce the heat to a simmer, and cook, uncovered,
for 20 minutes until reduced to a thick sauce. Use a hand-held
blender or food processor to blend it until smooth. Cool.

3 Rub the pork in the sauce, cover, and marinate in the fridge for at
least 4 hours, but preferably overnight. Preheat the oven to 180°C
(350°F/Gas 4). Put the pork and marinade in an oven tray just big
enough to fit it. Put a piece of greaseproof paper over the top (to stop
the skin sticking to the foil) and seal with a double layer
of foil. Cook the pork for 2½ hours.

4 Prepare a barbecue for cooking. Remove the meat from the oven.
Pat the skin dry with kitchen paper and rub in a little oil, then some
salt. Grill it over a hot barbecue for 10–15 minutes on each side,
skin-side down first; carefully turn with tongs, but do not turn it until
the crackling is crispy and charred in places.

5 Meanwhile, pour the juices from the oven tray into a saucepan and
first pour, then skim off all the fat. Reduce the sauce over a medium
heat to a thick pouring consistency.

6 Cut the crackling off the meat and leave it uncovered (or it will go
soft) while you rest the meat wrapped in foil for 10 minutes. When
ready to serve, cut the crackling into shards. Shred the pork into a
juicy pile, pour over the sauce, and serve, with the wraps and
accompaniments.

Nutrition data per serving

Energy	335kcals/1411kJ
Carbohydrate	7g
of which sugar	7g
Fat	12g
of which saturates	3.5g
Salt	1.1g
Fibre	0.4g

Spicy pork and beans

This is a sort of cowboy-style barbecue pork and beans,
rich with dark, smoky flavours.

INGREDIENTS

150g (5½oz) mixed dried
  beans, such as black-eyed,
  black, and cannellini beans,
  soaked overnight
2 tbsp olive oil
2 onions, finely chopped
2 garlic cloves, crushed
2 tsp plain flour
2 tsp smoked paprika
salt and freshly ground
  black pepper
500g (1lb 2oz) pork shoulder,
  cut into 3cm (1in) cubes
½ tsp dried oregano
1 tsp dark brown sugar
500ml (16fl oz) beef stock
2 tbsp good-quality
  barbecue sauce
baked potatoes, to serve

SERVES 4 **PREP 20 MINS, PLUS SOAKING** **COOK 2 HRS 15 MINS**

1 Place the beans in a saucepan with plenty of fresh water. Bring to the boil over a high heat and simmer for 10 minutes. Drain and refresh under cold water. Set aside.

2 Heat 1 tbsp of the oil in a large, heavy-based saucepan. Fry the onions over a medium heat for 5 minutes. Add the garlic and cook for a further minute. Set aside.

3 Put the flour in a freezer bag with 1 tsp of the smoked paprika and salt and pepper. Toss the pork in it. Tip out into a sieve, shaking to remove excess flour.

4 Fry the pork in the remaining 1 tbsp of oil, in batches, for a couple of minutes on each side.

5 Return the onion mixture and stir in the remaining 1 tsp of smoked paprika, the oregano, and sugar. Mix in the stock and barbecue sauce and bring to the boil. Reduce to a gentle simmer and cook, covered, for 1 hour.

6 Add the beans, cover, and cook for 30 minutes. Uncover and cook for 30 minutes, adding water if needed, until the beans and pork are tender. Serve with baked potatoes.

Nutrition data per serving

Energy	400kcals/1691kJ
Carbohydrate	32g
of which sugar	8g
Fat	11.5g
of which saturates	3g
Salt	0.8g
Fibre	6.5g

Spaghetti alle vongole

The classic Italian dish is made with fresh clams, but this
version uses a can for a storecupboard supper.

....

INGREDIENTS

3 tbsp olive oil
1 onion, finely chopped
2 garlic cloves, crushed
280g can clams
400g can chopped tomatoes
1 tbsp tomato purée
1 tsp caster sugar
2 tbsp roughly chopped
   flat-leaf parsley leaves
salt and freshly ground
   black pepper
300g (10oz) dried spaghetti

SERVES 4   **PREP** 15 MINS   **COOK** 1 HR 5 MINS

1 Heat 2 tbsp of the oil in a heavy-based saucepan, and cook the onion
over a medium heat for about 5 minutes, until softened, but not
browned. Add the garlic and cook for a minute. Drain the clams,
reserving the liquid. Cover and refrigerate the clams.

2 Add the tomatoes and clam liquid to the onions. Stir in the tomato
purée, sugar, and parsley, and season well. Bring to the boil, reduce
the heat to a low simmer, and cook for about 1 hour until thickened and
reduced. If the tomatoes are taking a while to break down, mash with
a potato masher to help them along.

3 When the sauce is nearly ready, cook the spaghetti in a large pan
of boiling salted water according to the packet instructions. Drain
the spaghetti (reserving a ladleful of the cooking water), and return
it to the pan with the reserved water.

4 Add the clams and remaining oil to the sauce and allow to heat
through, before tossing in the cooked spaghetti.

Nutrition data per serving	
Energy	387kcals/1634kJ
Carbohydrate	59g
of which sugar	8.5g
Fat	10g
of which saturates	1.5g
Salt	0.3g
Fibre	5g

Roast chicken and roots

Cooking a whole chicken in a tin of colourful root vegetables will give you a convenient and healthy meal in one.

INGREDIENTS

1 good-quality chicken,
  1.5–2kg (3lb 3oz–4½lb)

4 large potatoes, peeled
  and quartered

3 large carrots, cut into
  3cm (1in) chunks

2 parsnips, cut into
  3cm (1in) chunks

2 leeks, white part only, cut
  into 3cm (1in) chunks

2 tbsp olive oil

salt and freshly ground
  black pepper

1 tbsp butter, softened

½ lemon

100ml (3½fl oz) white wine
  or chicken stock

SERVES 4-6   **PREP** 20 MINS   **COOK** 1 HR 15 MINS, PLUS RESTING

1 Preheat the oven to 200°C (400°F/Gas 6). Wipe the skin of the chicken dry with kitchen paper. Undo the string and work the legs away from the body slightly.

2 Put the vegetables in a large roasting tin, toss them with the oil, and season well. Push them to the sides of the tin to make room for the chicken.

3 Rub the chicken all over with the butter and season it well. Put the chicken into the space you made in the roasting tin, surrounded by the vegetables. (Do not put it on top, or the vegetables may cook unevenly.) Squeeze the half lemon over the breast, then put the squeezed-out lemon shell inside the cavity.

4 Pour the wine or stock around the vegetables and roast in the oven for about 1¼ hours, turning the vegetables occasionally, or until the chicken juices run clear when you insert a skewer into the thickest part of the thigh.

5 Rest the chicken for 10 minutes, lightly covered with foil. Pour any juices that come from the chicken back into the vegetables, then carve the chicken and serve with the vegetables and juices.

Cook's tip: Roasting the vegetables with the chicken will soak up a lot of the chicken juices, and not leave much for a gravy. Try serving it with a "wet" vegetable such as slow-cooked Savoy cabbage.

Nutrition data per serving

Energy	444kcals/1868kJ
Carbohydrate	37g
of which sugar	9g
Fat	11g
of which saturates	3g
Salt	0.4g
Fibre	8.5g

Spicy chicken meatballs

These are perfect alongside a vegetable and noodle stir-fry.
Finely chopped chilli can be added for more heat.

INGREDIENTS

400g (14oz) minced chicken

50g (1¾oz) fresh white
breadcrumbs

2 spring onions,
finely chopped

1 garlic clove, crushed

2cm (¾in) fresh root ginger,
finely grated

1 tbsp finely chopped
coriander leaves

1 tbsp sweet chilli sauce

1 tsp lime juice

1 tsp fish sauce

2 tbsp sunflower oil

SERVES 4

PREP 10 MINS, PLUS CHILLING

COOK 10 MINS

1 Mix all the ingredients, except the oil, together in a large bowl until evenly incorporated. It's easiest to use your fingers for this; you may prefer to wear plastic food preparation gloves. Cover and refrigerate for at least 30 minutes.

2 With damp hands, shape walnut-sized balls with the chicken mixture, placing them on a plate. At this point, you may cover and chill the meatballs for up to 1 day, if that is more convenient.

3 Heat the sunflower oil in a large frying pan and fry the meatballs over a medium-high heat for about 3–5 minutes, turning to colour all sides, until golden and cooked through (cut one through to the centre to check there is no trace of pink). You may need to do this in batches, depending on the size of the pan. Serve.

Nutrition data per serving

Energy	211kcals/888kJ
Carbohydrate	11.5g
of which sugar	3g
Fat	7g
of which saturates	1g
Salt	0.8g
Fibre	0.5g

Hot spiced rice with chicken and pomegranate

The heady spice mix elevates this easy chicken dish –
plus it's a real feast for the eyes!

INGREDIENTS

¹/₂ tsp ground cinnamon

¹/₂ tsp ground allspice

¹/₂ tsp ground cloves

¹/₂ tsp ground coriander

salt and freshly ground
black pepper

juice of 1 orange

150ml (5fl oz) pomegranate
juice (see Cook's tip)

2 garlic cloves, finely chopped

8 chicken thighs, skin on

3 courgettes, thickly sliced

300g (10oz) basmati rice

1–2 Scotch bonnet chillies,
left whole

150g (5¹/₂oz) pomegranate
seeds, or seeds from 1
pomegranate

SERVES 4 **PREP** 15 MINS, PLUS MARINATING **COOK** 35-40 MINS

1 Preheat the oven to 200°C (400°F/Gas 6). Mix all the spices with the salt and pepper, orange juice, pomegranate juice, and garlic. Place the chicken pieces in a roasting tin and pour over half the mixture to coat. Cover and marinate for 30 minutes, then roast in the oven for 20–25 minutes. Add the courgettes to the roasting tin and cook for another 15 minutes or until the chicken is golden and the skin begins to char slightly.

2 Meanwhile, place the rice and chillies in a pan, and top up with water so it just covers the rice. Season with salt and tip in the remaining spice mix. Cook on a medium heat with the lid ajar for 15 minutes until the rice has absorbed all the water and is just cooked. Turn off the heat, sit the lid on top, and leave for 10 minutes to steam.

3 Transfer the rice to a serving dish, top with the chicken and any juices, and the courgettes, and sprinkle with the pomegranate seeds to serve. Use Scotch bonnets for garnish, or chop and scatter over the dish for some heat.

Cook's tip: Make fresh pomegranate juice by squashing the seeds from 3 fresh pomegranates through a sieve. Alternatively, try pomegranate molasses for a more intense flavour.

Nutrition data per serving

Energy	518kcals/2174kJ
Carbohydrate	68g
of which sugar	13g
Fat	8g
of which saturates	2g
Salt	0.35g
Fibre	2g

Stir-fried chicken and asparagus

The mild spicing in this dish complements the delicate flavour of the asparagus.

INGREDIENTS

2 tsp cornflour

3 tbsp soy sauce

2 tbsp rice wine or dry sherry

2 tsp caster sugar

500g (1lb 2oz) skinless boneless chicken thighs, finely sliced

1 bunch of asparagus, woody ends removed, cut into 3cm (1in) pieces, stalks and tips separated

salt

2 tbsp sunflower oil

2 garlic cloves, finely chopped

4cm (1½in) fresh root ginger, finely chopped

1 bunch of spring onions, cut into 3cm (1in) pieces

rice, to serve

SERVES 4   **PREP 15 MINS, PLUS MARINATING**   **COOK 10 MINS**

1 Mix together 1 tsp of the cornflour, 1 tbsp of the soy sauce, 1 tbsp of the rice wine, and 1 tsp of the sugar in a large bowl. Toss through the chicken, cover, and refrigerate for 30 minutes.

2 Meanwhile, cook the asparagus stalks in a pan of boiling salted water for 1 minute, then add the tips and blanch for a further minute. Drain and refresh under cold water. Mix the remaining cornflour with 1 tbsp of cold water. Set aside.

3 Heat the oil in a wok and, when it is hot, add the garlic and ginger and fry for 1 minute. Add the chicken and stir-fry for 3–4 minutes. Add the spring onions and cook for a further 2 minutes.

4 Add the remaining soy sauce, rice wine, sugar, and 2 tbsp of water, and bring to the boil.

5 Stir and add the cornflour mixture, then the asparagus. Cook for a further 2 minutes until the mixture thickens and the asparagus is hot. Serve over rice.

Nutrition data per serving

Energy	241kcals/1008kJ
Carbohydrate	8g
of which sugar	6g
Fat	9.5g
of which saturates	1.5g
Salt	2.3g
Fibre	2g

Chicken cacciatore

Chicken breasts can be dry. Cooking them in this rich, Italian sauce will give them a succulent texture.

INGREDIENTS

1 tbsp olive oil
4 skin-on bone-in chicken breasts
1 red onion, finely chopped
2 garlic cloves, finely chopped
1 red pepper, sliced
2 x 400g cans cherry tomatoes
200ml (7fl oz) chicken stock
1/2 tsp dried rosemary
75g (2 1/2oz) pitted black olives
salt and freshly ground
    black pepper
basil leaves, to garnish
pasta or boiled rice, to serve

SERVES 4   **PREP 10 MINS**   **COOK 50-55 MINS**

1 Preheat the oven to 190°C (375°F/Gas 5). Place half the oil in a large, heavy-based flameproof casserole over a medium heat and brown the chicken on all sides. Remove with a slotted spoon and set aside on a plate lined with kitchen paper.

2 Add the remaining oil and fry the onion for 5 minutes, stirring occasionally. Add the garlic and pepper, and fry for a further 2 minutes. Add the tomatoes, stock, rosemary, and olives, season well, and stir.

3 Return the chicken and coat in the sauce. Bring to the boil, cover, and bake in the oven for 30–35 minutes, or until the chicken is cooked. Sprinkle with basil and serve with pasta or boiled rice.

Nutrition data per serving

Energy	301kcals/1267kJ
Carbohydrate	10g
of which sugar	9g
Fat	10g
of which saturates	2g
Salt	0.8g
Fibre	4g

Spicy turkey burgers

Try making small versions of these Asian-inspired burgers
as a canapé served with sweet chilli sauce.

INGREDIENTS

400g (14oz) minced turkey

75g (2¹/₂oz) fresh white
breadcrumbs

1 tbsp sweet chilli sauce

4 spring onions, white part
only, finely sliced

4 tbsp finely chopped
coriander leaves

2cm (³/₄in) fresh root
ginger, finely grated

1 red chilli, deseeded and
finely chopped

salt and freshly ground
black pepper

To serve

4 burger buns

lettuce

tomato

finely sliced red onions

mayonnaise

Greek yogurt

sweet chilli sauce

SERVES 4   **PREP** 15 MINS, PLUS CHILLING   **COOK** 10 MINS

1 Prepare a barbecue for cooking. In a large bowl, mix together all the ingredients until well combined.

2 With damp hands (to help stop the mixture sticking to your fingers), divide the mixture into 4 balls and roll each one between your palms until smooth. Flatten each ball out to a large, fat disk, 3cm (1in) high, and pat the edges in to tidy them up. Place the burgers on a plate, cover with cling film, and chill for 30 minutes (this helps them keep their shape on cooking).

3 Cook over a hot barbecue for 6–7 minutes, turning as needed, until the meat is springy to the touch and the edges charred.

4 Serve with a selection of buns and accompaniments, and let everyone build their own burgers.

Nutrition data per serving	
Energy	244kcals/1027kJ
Carbohydrate	16g
of which sugar	2.5g
Fat	7g
of which saturates	3g
Salt	0.5g
Fibre	0.8g

Falafel burgers with rocket and tzatziki

These vegetarian burgers make a great alternative to a traditional burger, and are quick and easy to make.

INGREDIENTS

For the falafel

400g can cooked chickpeas

75g (2½oz) fresh breadcrumbs

1 small egg, beaten

2 large spring onions, trimmed and finely chopped

1 large garlic clove, crushed

2 tbsp plain flour

2 heaped tbsp each of roughly chopped flat-leaf parsley, fresh coriander, and mint

½ tsp each of ground cumin and coriander

salt and freshly ground black pepper

2 tbsp olive oil

For the tzatziki

170g (6oz) low-fat Greek-style yogurt

1 garlic clove, crushed

handful of mint leaves, finely chopped

To serve

4 fresh pitta breads

70g (2¼oz) bag of rocket

1 lemon, quartered

SERVES 4   **PREP 15 MINS, PLUS CHILLING**   **COOK 8 MINS**

1 For the falafel, drain and rinse the chickpeas and place all the ingredients, except the oil, in a food processor and process to form a rough paste. Roll the mixture into 4 balls and flatten them to make 1.5cm (³/₄in) thick patties. Cover and chill in the fridge for 30 minutes, to help the patties hold together when cooking.

2 Heat the olive oil in a large, non-stick frying pan. Fry the patties, over a low heat, for 3–4 minutes on each side, until golden brown and crispy on the outside and cooked through.

3 For the tzatziki, mix together the yogurt, garlic, and mint, and season well. Heat or toast the pitta bread slightly to soften it (this can be done in a toaster), then use a small, sharp knife to split one side to make a pocket. Stuff each pitta pocket with a quarter of the rocket leaves and a falafel patty. Top with a little of the tzatziki, to taste. Serve the burgers with some lemon squeezed over, and hot sauce, if you prefer.

Nutrition data per serving

Energy		454kcals/1900kJ
Carbohydrate		71g
of which sugar		5g
Fat		10.5g
of which saturates		2g
Salt		1.6g
Fibre		6g

Sweet potato and aubergine curry

Keep jars of good curry pastes in your storecupboard and you'll always be able to rustle up a quick, tasty meal.

INGREDIENTS

salt and freshly ground
  black pepper
400g (14oz) potatoes, peeled and
  cut into 2cm (¾in) cubes
400g (14oz) sweet potatoes, peeled
  and cut into 2cm (¾in) cubes
1 tbsp vegetable oil
1 onion, finely chopped
2 garlic cloves, finely chopped
1 aubergine, cut into
  2cm (¾in) cubes
4 tbsp mild curry paste
  (such as korma)
400g can chopped tomatoes
250ml (9fl oz) vegetable stock
3 tbsp chopped coriander leaves
basmati rice and plain yogurt,
  to serve

SERVES 4   **PREP** 15 MINS   **COOK** 30 MINS

1 Bring a saucepan of salted water to the boil, add the potato and sweet potato, and cook for 10 minutes. Drain and set aside.

2 Meanwhile, heat the oil in a large pan over a medium heat and fry the onion for 5 minutes. Add the garlic and aubergine and cook for a further 2 minutes.

3 Add the curry paste to the pan and stir well. Add the tomatoes, stock, and cooked potatoes, and stir to combine. Season, cover, and simmer for 20 minutes.

4 Stir in the coriander. Serve the curry with rice and topped with a spoonful of yogurt.

Nutrition data per serving	
Energy	258kcals/1089kJ
Carbohydrate	43g
of which sugar	11g
Fat	7g
of which saturates	0.5g
Salt	0.8g
Fibre	8g

Pasta with butternut squash

This dish is perfect for those slightly cooler days, as it has the comfort of cream and the warmth of red chillies.

INGREDIENTS

200g (7oz) butternut squash, peeled and diced

1 tbsp olive oil

salt and freshly ground black pepper

1 garlic clove, crushed

1/2 red chilli, deseeded and finely chopped

8 sage leaves

150ml (5fl oz) single cream

25g (scant 1oz) Parmesan cheese, grated, plus extra to serve

350g (12oz) dried conchiglie pasta or other pasta shapes

SERVES 4   **PREP** 20 MINS   **COOK** 30 MINS

1 Preheat the oven to 200°C (400°F/Gas 6). Toss the squash in a little oil, season it well with salt and pepper, and roast for about 30 minutes, or until soft. Remove it from the oven and leave to cool for a few minutes.

2 Meanwhile, gently fry the garlic, chilli, and sage in a little oil for 2–3 minutes.

3 Once the butternut squash has cooled slightly, put it into a blender or food processor. Add the cream, Parmesan, garlic, chilli, sage leaves, plenty of pepper, and a little salt. Blend it all to a coarse purée, adding 1–2 tbsp water if it looks too thick.

4 Cook the pasta until al dente and drain it. Quickly reheat the sauce in the pasta pan, adding more water if it seems a little stiff. Put the pasta back into the pan and mix it well, allowing the sauce to coat the pasta. Serve with a small sprinkling of Parmesan.

Nutrition data per serving

Energy	451kcals/1906kJ
Carbohydrate	66g
of which sugar	5g
Fat	14g
of which saturates	7g
Salt	0.2g
Fibre	5g

Vegetable biryani

This tasty Indian dish is packed full of vegetables, and the cashew nuts add protein for vegetarians, too.

INGREDIENTS

400g (14oz) white basmati rice

salt and freshly ground black pepper

2 tbsp vegetable oil

1 large onion, finely chopped

2.5cm (1in) piece of fresh root ginger, finely chopped

2 garlic cloves, finely chopped

1 tsp ground coriander

2 tsp ground cumin

1 tsp turmeric

1/2–1 tsp chilli powder

900ml (1 1/2 pints) vegetable stock

2 sweet potatoes, peeled and finely chopped

200g (7oz) fine green beans, halved

200g (7oz) small cauliflower florets

1 tsp garam masala

juice of 1 lemon

handful of coriander leaves, chopped

50g (1 3/4oz) unsalted cashew nuts

raita, to serve

SERVES 4-6　**PREP 20-30 MINS**　**COOK 40-45 MINS**

1 Rinse the rice, then tip into a large pan of salted water, and cook according to the packet instructions. Drain, and set aside.

2 Meanwhile, heat the oil in a large pan over a medium heat and fry the onion for 5 minutes. Add the ginger and garlic and fry for 2 minutes. Add the spices and fry for 1 minute, stirring.

3 Stir in the stock, season, and bring to the boil. Add the sweet potatoes, cover, and simmer for 10 minutes. Stir in the beans and cauliflower and cook for a further 10 minutes.

4 Return the rice to heat through. Stir in the garam masala and lemon juice. Season to taste and stir in the coriander and nuts. Serve with raita.

Nutrition data per serving	
Energy	621kcals/2598kJ
Carbohydrate	102g
of which sugar	10g
Fat	13g
of which saturates	2g
Salt	0.2g
Fibre	7g

One-pot Indian rice

One-pot meals are a real lifesaver when time is short but
you want to produce an enjoyable family meal.

INGREDIENTS

1 tbsp vegetable oil
1 onion, finely chopped
2 garlic cloves, finely chopped
1 red pepper, finely chopped
1 green pepper, finely chopped
4 tbsp medium curry powder
250g (9oz) white basmati rice
500ml (16fl oz) vegetable stock
salt and freshly ground
    black pepper
30g (1oz) toasted flaked almonds
250g (9oz) cooked prawns,
    shelled and deveined
150g (5¹/₂oz) plain low-fat yogurt
2 tbsp finely chopped mint leaves
2 tbsp finely chopped
    coriander leaves

SERVES 4   **PREP 15 MINS**   **COOK 25 MINS**

1 Heat the oil in a heavy-based saucepan over a medium heat and cook the onion for 5 minutes.

2 Add the garlic and peppers and cook for 1 minute. Stir in the curry powder and rice and cook for 1 minute, stirring constantly.

3 Stir in the stock, season well, and bring to the boil. Cover and simmer over a low heat for 12–15 minutes. When the rice is nearly cooked, stir in the almonds and prawns to heat through.

4 Meanwhile, place the yogurt in a small serving bowl and stir in the herbs. Set aside.

5 Serve the rice on warmed plates with a dollop of the mint and coriander yogurt on top.

Nutrition data per serving	
Energy	442kcals/1847kJ
Carbohydrate	56g
of which sugar	9g
Fat	11.5g
of which saturates	1.5g
Salt	0.2g
Fibre	2g

Turkish-style stuffed peppers

A good dish to make use of leftover rice.

INGREDIENTS

125g (4½oz) basmati rice

1 tbsp olive oil, plus extra
for drizzling

1 red onion, peeled and
finely chopped

salt and freshly ground
black pepper

1 garlic clove, finely chopped

small handful of flat-leaf parsley,
finely chopped

small handful of fresh thyme
leaves, chopped

pinch of dried oregano

1 tomato, diced

½ tsp paprika

2 tsp pine nuts, toasted (see
Cook's tip)

1 tbsp pitted and chopped
black olives

2 red peppers, tops removed
and retained, seeds removed

SERVES 2    **PREP 15 MINS**   **COOK 45–50 MINS**

1 First cook the rice according to pack instructions, drain and put to one side. Preheat the oven to 200°C (400°F/Gas 6).

2 Heat the olive oil in a frying pan, add the onion and season with salt and black pepper. Cook over a low heat for 3–4 minutes until soft, add the garlic and cook for a few seconds more, then remove from the heat and allow to cool. Stir in the herbs, tomato, paprika, pine nuts, and olives, then add the cooked rice and stir again. Taste and season if needed.

3 Spoon the mixture into the peppers, packing them tightly so they hold together while cooking. Place them upright in a roasting tin, topped with the lids, drizzle with olive oil, and cook for 30–45 minutes until the peppers begin to soften and char slightly. Cover with foil towards the end of cooking if the rice is beginning to dry out too much. Serve hot.

Cook's tip: Toast the pine nuts on a baking sheet in a hot oven or in a small dry frying pan over a moderate heat. Cook for a few minutes, keeping a close eye on them to make sure they don't burn.

Nutrition data per serving

Energy	535kcals/1475kJ
Carbohydrate	67g
of which sugar	14.5g
Fat	6g
of which saturates	0.5g
Salt	0.2g
Fibre	4g

Pasta with roasted fennel

Roasted fennel, partnered by sweet cherry tomatoes,
adds a stylish flair to spaghetti or linguine.

INGREDIENTS

2 fennel bulbs, trimmed and
sliced lengthways
salt and freshly ground
black pepper
250g (9oz) cherry
tomatoes, halved
2 tbsp olive oil
1 red onion, finely chopped
2 garlic cloves, finely chopped
350g (12oz) spaghetti or linguine
1 tbsp flat-leaf parsley,
finely chopped

SERVES 4   **PREP** 10 MINS   **COOK** 30 MINS

1 Preheat the oven to 200°C (400°F/Gas 6). Put the fennel in a pan of salted boiling water, bring back to the boil and cook for about 5 minutes until softened, then drain well.

2 Turn the fennel into a roasting tin, add the tomatoes, drizzle with half the olive oil and sprinkle with salt and black pepper. Combine thoroughly, using your hands. Roast in the oven for about 20 minutes or until soft and beginning to char very slightly.

3 Put a pan of salted water on to boil for the pasta. Meanwhile, heat the remaining oil in a frying pan, add the onion and cook for about 5 minutes until soft. Stir in the garlic and cook for a few more seconds, then remove the pan from the heat and set aside.

4 Cook the pasta in the boiling water for 8–10 minutes or according to the instructions on the packet. Drain, reserving some of the cooking water, then return the pasta to the pan with a little of the water. Toss together with the onion mixture, fennel, and tomatoes. Transfer to a serving dish (or dishes) and sprinkle with the parsley to serve.

Cook's tip: You don't have to boil the fennel first, but it does soften it and stops it from becoming too brittle when roasted.

Nutrition data per serving

Energy	382kcals/1617kJ
Carbohydrate	71g
of which sugar	6g
Fat	7.5g
of which saturates	1g
Salt	trace
Fibre	5g

Spaghetti with courgettes and toasted almonds

Lemony courgettes add a real zing to this quick pasta dish, which is sprinkled with crunchy toasted almonds.

INGREDIENTS

300g (10oz) spaghetti
2 tbsp olive oil
2 courgettes, diced
2 courgettes, grated
salt and freshly ground
    black pepper
2 garlic cloves, finely chopped
juice of 1 lemon
pinch of dried oregano
25g (scant 1oz) flaked
    almonds, toasted
    (see Cook's tip)

SERVES 4   **PREP** 10 MINS   **COOK** 15 MINS

1 Cook the pasta in a large pan of salted boiling water for 8–10 minutes, or according to the instructions on the packet.

2 Meanwhile, heat the olive oil in a large frying pan. Add all the courgettes, together with a pinch of salt and some black pepper. Cook for 5–8 minutes until soft and just beginning to turn golden at the edges. Stir in the garlic and cook for a few more seconds, then add the lemon juice and oregano and simmer for about 5 minutes.

3 Drain the pasta, reserving some of the cooking water, then return it to the pan with a little of the water. Add the courgette mixture and toss well. Transfer to a serving dish, or dishes, and top with the toasted almonds.

Cook's tip: To toast the almonds, tip them onto a baking tray and place it in the oven, which has been preheated to 200°C (400°F/Gas 6). Cook for 3–5 minutes until golden, turning them halfway through cooking. Alternatively, cook them in a small frying pan for a few minutes until golden, stirring occasionally so they don't burn.

Nutrition data per serving

Energy	362kcals/1528kJ
Carbohydrate	58g
of which sugar	4g
Fat	11g
of which saturates	1g
Salt	trace
Fibre	3.5g

Lentils with turnips and chestnuts

A chunky vegetable dish with versatility: serve
it as a soup or a casserole.

INGREDIENTS

1 tbsp olive oil

1 onion, finely chopped

salt and freshly ground
    black pepper

2 garlic cloves, finely chopped

2 turnips, cut into chunks

200g vacuum pack of chestnuts

3 sage leaves, roughly chopped

1 tbsp fresh parsley,
    roughly chopped

350g (12oz) Puy lentils, rinsed
    and any grit removed

1.2 litres (2 pints) vegetable stock

SERVES 4   **PREP** 10 MINS   **COOK** 50 MINS

1 Heat the oil in a large, heavy pan, add the onion and cook until soft. Season with salt and black pepper, then stir in the garlic, turnips, chestnuts, sage, and parsley.

2 Stir in the lentils so they are coated with the vegetable mixture, then pour in the stock and bring to the boil. Reduce to a simmer, partially cover the pan and cook gently for about 40 minutes or until the lentils are soft, topping up with more stock if needed.

3 Season to taste, then ladle into bowls and serve.

Nutrition data per serving	
Energy	442kcals/1872kJ
Carbohydrate	67g
of which sugar	8g
Fat	8g
of which saturates	1.5g
Salt	1.4g
Fibre	11g

Kasha with vegetables

Added vegetables and goat's cheese make this kasha dish a hearty vegetarian main course.

INGREDIENTS

2 tbsp olive oil

1 onion, finely chopped

1 carrot, finely chopped

1 garlic clove, finely chopped

2 flat mushrooms, sliced

1 celery stick, finely chopped

550g (1¼lb) kasha

120ml (4fl oz) dry white wine

1.2 litres (2 pints) hot vegetable stock or water

1 beetroot, steamed or roasted until tender, chopped

2 tbsp chopped parsley

60g (2oz) goat's cheese, crumbled

SERVES 4   **PREP 10 MINS**   **COOK 40 MINS**

1 Heat the oil in a large saucepan. Add the onion, carrot, garlic, mushrooms, and celery and sauté for 8–10 minutes, stirring frequently, until brown. Add the kasha and cook, stirring for another 2–3 minutes. Add the wine and continue stirring until all the liquid has been absorbed.

2 Gradually add the hot vegetable stock, 120ml (4fl oz) at a time, and stirring until it has been absorbed before adding more. Cook for a further 20 minutes, or until the kasha is soft and chewy.

3 Toss in the chopped cooked beetroot and remove from the heat. Sprinkle over the parsley and goat's cheese, and serve.

Nutrition data per serving

Energy	362kcals/1521kJ
Carbohydrate	55g
of which sugar	8g
Fat	11.5g
of which saturates	4g
Salt	0.7g
Fibre	4.5g

SNACKS
AND SWEETS

Multi-seed crackers

These can be adapted using a mixture of the seeds you like.
Be sure to use the larger seeds for decorating.

INGREDIENTS

150g (5½oz) wholemeal flour

75g (2½oz) plain flour, plus
    extra for dusting

50g (1¾oz) butter, in pieces,
    softened

½ tsp fine salt

2 tbsp sesame seeds

2 tbsp linseeds

2 tbsp pumpkin seeds, plus
    extra for decorating

2 tbsp sunflower seeds, plus
    extra for decorating

1 tbsp clear honey

1 egg white

MAKES 45-50   **PREP** 20 MINS   **COOK** 12-15 MINS

1 Preheat the oven to 200°C (400°F/Gas 6). In a large bowl with your fingertips, or in a food processor using the pulse-blend setting, blend the flours, butter, and salt until the mixture resembles fine crumbs. Mix in all the seeds.

2 Dissolve the honey in 100ml (3½fl oz) of warm water. Make a well in the flour and mix in the water to form a soft dough.

3 Turn the dough onto a floured surface and knead it briefly. Roll out as thinly as possible – aim for 1–2mm (½₄–½₁₂in) thick.

4 Cut the dough into 4 x 6cm (1½ x 2½in) crackers. Leave on the work surface.

5 Whisk the egg white with ½ tbsp of water and brush the crackers. Scatter the additional pumpkin and sunflower seeds over, and gently press in.

6 Transfer to 2 baking sheets using a fish slice, and bake for 12–15 minutes, turning carefully halfway, or until both sides are crisp and golden brown. Leave to cool on their trays. Store in an airtight container for up to 2 weeks.

Nutrition data per serving	
Energy	38kcals/157kJ
Carbohydrate	3g
of which sugar	0.4g
Fat	2g
of which saturates	0.8g
Salt	trace
Fibre	0.7g

Pumpkin, feta, and rosemary rolls

A herby, cheesy twist on soda bread, these simple rolls are perfect with a home-made soup, freeze well, and make a satisfying snack after school.

INGREDIENTS

200g (7oz) plain flour
200g (7oz) wholemeal flour
1¹/₂ tsp finely chopped rosemary
1 tsp bicarbonate of soda
¹/₂ tsp fine salt and freshly ground black pepper
100g (3¹/₂oz) pumpkin or butternut squash, peeled and coarsely grated
100g (3¹/₂oz) feta cheese, crumbled
300ml (10fl oz) buttermilk

MAKES 8   **PREP** 20 MINS   **COOK** 20-25 MINS

1 Preheat oven to 200°C (400°F/Gas 6). Sift both lots of flour into a large bowl. Mix in the rosemary, bicarbonate of soda, salt, and a good grinding of black pepper.

2 Toss the grated pumpkin and feta through the flour mixture. Make a well in the centre and pour in the buttermilk. Use a wooden spoon and then your hands to bring the mixture together to form a rough dough.

3 On a lightly floured surface, knead the dough very briefly, until it is a smooth ball. Cut it into 8 equal-sized wedges and form each into a roll, with any joins underneath the roll.

4 Bake the rolls in the centre of the oven for 20–25 minutes, until golden brown. The bottom of the rolls should sound hollow when tapped. Remove from the oven and allow to cool for at least 10 minutes before serving.

Cook's tip: Make double the amount of dough and open freeze half the rolls, unbaked, on a tray. Then pack them in a freezer bag for storage. These can be baked straight from the freezer for 40 minutes.

Nutrition data per serving	
Energy	212kcals/878kJ
Carbohydrate	37g
of which sugar	3.5g
Fat	3.5g
of which saturates	2g
Salt	1.1g
Fibre	4g

Grissini

Tradition has it that breadsticks should be pulled to the length
of the baker's arm... these are more manageable!

INGREDIENTS

2½ tsp dried yeast

425g (15oz) strong white bread
flour, plus extra for dusting

1 tbsp caster sugar

2 tsp salt

2 tbsp extra virgin olive oil

45g (1½oz) sesame seeds

MAKES 32

PREP 40-45 MINS,
PLUS RISING

COOK 15-18 MINS

1 Sprinkle the yeast over 4 tbsp of warm water. Leave for 5 minutes, stirring once. Put the flour, sugar, and salt in a bowl. Add the yeast, 250ml (9fl oz) of warm water, and the oil. Mix to make a sticky dough.

2 Knead on a floured surface for 5–7 minutes until very smooth and elastic. Let rest for 5 minutes.

3 Roll the dough out to 40 x 15cm (16 x 6in). Cover it with a damp tea towel. Leave in a warm place for 1½ hours, until doubled in size.

4 Preheat the oven to 220°C (425°F/Gas 7). Dust 3 baking sheets with flour. Brush the dough with water and sprinkle with the sesame seeds.

5 With a sharp knife, cut the dough into 32 strips, each 1cm (½in) wide. Stretch 1 strip to the width of a baking sheet. Set it on the baking sheet. Repeat with the remaining strips, arranging them 2cm (¾in) apart. Bake for 15–18 minutes until golden and crisp. These keep in an airtight container for up to 2 days.

Nutrition data per serving	
Energy	63kcals/266kJ
Carbohydrate	10g
of which sugar	1g
Fat	2g
of which saturates	0.5g
Salt	0.2g
Fibre	0.5g

Mini falafel

These tasty little falafel are perfect for buffet
lunches or as a healthy snack.

INGREDIENTS

400g can of chickpeas, drained,
    and rinsed
4 tbsp fresh breadcrumbs
1 egg yolk
1/2 onion, finely chopped
1 garlic clove, crushed
2 tbsp plain flour
2 tbsp finely chopped
    flat-leaf parsley
1 tbsp sunflower oil
low fat hummus, and cucumber
    and carrot sticks, to serve

MAKES 10-12   **PREP** 10 MINS, PLUS CHILLING   **COOK** 30 MINS, PLUS COOLING

1 Place all the ingredients except the oil into a food processor and
process it to a rough paste. Roll the mixture into 10–12 walnut-sized
balls, cover, and chill for 30 minutes.

2 Preheat the oven to 200°C (400°F/Gas 6). Grease a heavy baking
tray with the oil and heat in the oven for a couple of minutes. Lay
the falafel on the tray, spaced apart, and cook for 15 minutes, until
they start to brown underneath.

3 Turn carefully and cook for a further 15 minutes, until brown
and crispy all over.

4 Cool on kitchen paper for 5 minutes. Serve with hummus,
and cucumber and carrot sticks.

Nutrition data per serving

Energy	65kcals/274kJ
Carbohydrate	8g
of which sugar	0.5g
Fat	2g
of which saturates	0.3g
Salt	0.2g
Fibre	1.8g

Root vegetable chips

These delicious, healthy roasted roots are perfect finger foods. Try other root vegetables or even some fruit, such as apples or pears.

INGREDIENTS

1 parsnip
1 sweet potato
1 carrot
1 tbsp sunflower oil

SERVES 4   **PREP 5 MINS**   **COOK 30 MINS**

1 Preheat the oven to 200°C (400°F/Gas 6). Peel all the vegetables and cut them into similar-sized wedges or fingers, so they cook evenly.

2 Toss the vegetable chips in the oil, and spread out in a single layer on a baking tray.

3 Cook for 25–30 minutes, turning them halfway, until they are well cooked and browning at the edges.

Nutrition data per serving	
Energy	101kcals/426kJ
Carbohydrate	15g
of which sugar	6.5g
Fat	3.5g
of which saturates	0.5g
Salt	trace
Fibre	3.5g

Sesame oatcakes

These oatcakes make a tasty and low-GI
alternative to crackers.

INGREDIENTS

85g (3oz) fine oatmeal
4 tbsp wholemeal flour
1 tbsp sesame seeds
scant 1/2 tsp salt
pinch of bicarbonate of soda
1 tbsp sesame oil

MAKES 9   **PREP** 5 MINS   **COOK** 10 MINS

1 Preheat the oven to
180°C (350°F/Gas 4).

2 Place the oatmeal, flour, sesame seeds, salt, and
bicarbonate of soda in a large bowl. Stir in the oil
and 75ml (2½fl oz) hot water to make a firm dough.

3 Roll the dough out on a lightly floured surface until
about 2mm thick and cut into circles using a 7.5cm (3in)
pastry cutter.

4 Bake for 8–10 minutes or until golden and crisp. Store in
an airtight container. Try with a low fat dip, such as hummus.

Nutrition data per serving

Energy	72kcals/303kJ
Carbohydrate	11.5g
of which sugar	0.1g
Fat	2g
of which saturates	0.2g
Salt	0.2g
Fibre	1g

Warm winter fruit salad

There's no need to miss out on fresh fruits in autumn
or winter; try them warm with a sweet syrup.

INGREDIENTS

85g (3oz) caster sugar

150ml (5fl oz) red wine

finely grated zest and juice of
1 orange, plus 2 oranges, peeled
and sliced into rounds

1 cinnamon stick

2 ripe pears, quartered, cored,
and peeled

4 plums, halved and pitted

SERVES 4   **PREP** 20 MINS   **COOK** 35 MINS

1 Place the sugar in a medium, heavy-based pan and add 300ml (10fl oz) of water. Place over a medium-low heat to dissolve the sugar. When it has all completely dissolved, increase the heat and bring it to the boil, then reduce the heat once more and simmer for 10 minutes.

2 Add the wine, orange zest and juice, and cinnamon stick to the pan and bring to the boil.

3 Reduce the heat and add the pears and plums. Cover and simmer over a medium heat for 10 minutes, or until the fruit is tender (test by piercing a big piece with a knife; it should meet no resistance). Stir in the orange slices.

4 Carefully remove the fruit from the pan using a slotted spoon, taking as little liquid as possible with the pieces, and set aside in a serving dish.

5 Boil the syrup over a high heat for 10 minutes to reduce it; it should thicken slightly. Remove the cinnamon stick from the syrup and pour it over the fruit. Serve warm or at room temperature.

Nutrition data per serving	
Energy	193kcals/819kJ
Carbohydrate	39g
of which sugar	40g
Fat	0g
of which saturates	0g
Salt	trace
Fibre	4.5g

Summer pudding

Make this classic, elegant dessert when summer fruits
are at their best, and serve with cream.

INGREDIENTS

550g (1¼lb) prepared mixed
  berries, such as raspberries,
  redcurrants, strawberries,
  blackcurrants, or blueberries,
  plus extra for serving
100g (3½oz) caster sugar
8 thin slices of white bread,
  crusts cut off

SERVES 4    **PREP 15 MINS,
PLUS CHILLING**   **COOK 5 MINS**

1 Place the fruit and sugar in a saucepan and add 3 tbsp of water.
  Heat until simmering and cook for 5 minutes.

2 Line a 900ml (1½ pint) pudding basin with 6 slices of the bread.
  Carefully spoon the fruit and all the juices into the lined bowl
and cover with the remaining bread, cutting to fit if necessary. Place
a saucer on top and then a 400g can to weigh it down. Place in the
fridge overnight.

3 Just before serving, remove the saucer and can and place a serving
  plate over the bowl. Invert the pudding onto the plate and top with
a few fresh berries, to decorate. Cut into wedges and serve.

Nutrition data per serving	
Energy	266kcals/1131kJ
Carbohydrate	57g
of which sugar	34g
Fat	1g
of which saturates	0.2g
Salt	0.7g
Fibre	5g

Traffic-light jellies

Fresh, sugar-free fruit juices make a healthier jelly. These take most of the day to set, but only minutes to make.

INGREDIENTS

1 packet of gelatine leaves
(12 x 1.75g leaves)

3 x 500ml cartons fresh fruit juice, such as pineapple, cranberry, kiwi, and apple (try to get different colours)

MAKES 10  **PREP** 15 MINS, PLUS SETTING **COOK** 5 MINS

1 Put 3 leaves of gelatine in a shallow bowl and cover them with cold water. Allow them to soften for 3–5 minutes until pliable.

2 Heat 1 fruit juice gently over a low heat in a small saucepan. When the gelatine is soft, remove it from the water and squeeze out the excess. Take the pan off the heat. Add the gelatine, whisking to dissolve. Cool, then divide equally between 10 small 150ml (5fl oz) plastic glasses. Chill to set.

3 Repeat the process with the second jelly, making sure you choose a contrasting colour to the first. Make sure the second fruit juice mixture is cold before pouring it carefully on top of the set jelly.

4 Repeat the process with the final fruit juice and return to the fridge to set before serving.

Nutrition data per serving

Energy	61kcals/260kJ
Carbohydrate	12g
of which sugar	12g
Fat	0g
of which saturates	0g
Salt	trace
Fibre	0.2g

Cranberry and pomegranate jelly

These tasty little jellies are perfect for occasions when
you fancy something sweet, but healthy.

INGREDIENTS

750ml (1¼ pints) light
    cranberry juice
1 tbsp powdered gelatine
    or vegetarian equivalent
2 pomegranates, seeds
    extracted and white
    membranes removed

SERVES 4  **PREP 10 MINS, PLUS SETTING** **COOK 5 MINS**

1 Place 120ml (4fl oz) of the cranberry juice in a small heatproof bowl, sprinkle in the gelatine and leave to soak for 5 minutes. Place the bowl over a pan of simmering water and stir until the gelatine melts and becomes clear. Stir in the remaining juice.

2 Divide the pomegranate seeds between 4 wine glasses, pour in enough of the liquid to just cover the fruit, and then chill for about 30 minutes or until just set.

3 Pour in the remaining liquid and chill for 3 hours, or until set.

Cook's tip: If the remaining cranberry juice mixture sets before you add it in the final step, place it over a pan of gently simmering water until it becomes liquid again.

Nutrition data per serving	
Energy	53kcals/221kJ
Carbohydrate	11g
of which sugar	11g
Fat	0g
of which saturates	0g
Salt	trace
Fibre	1g

Frozen fruity yogurt lollies

These summery treats are packed full of vitamin-rich
blueberries and have a lovely vivid colour.

INGREDIENTS

500g pot of plain yogurt
200g (7oz) blueberries
75g (2¹/₂oz) icing sugar

MAKES 6-8

 **PREP 5 MINS,
PLUS FREEZING**

1 Simply blend all the ingredients together in a blender, or using
a hand-held blender, until they are smooth, then freeze in lolly
moulds for up to 8 weeks.

2 Put the moulds carefully under running hot water for a minute
to help release the lollies when you are ready to serve them.

Nutrition data per serving	
Energy	100kcals/425kJ
Carbohydrate	16g
of which sugar	16g
Fat	2g
of which saturates	1g
Salt	0.1g
Fibre	0.3g

Sugar-free peach sorbet

A refreshing, melt-in-the-mouth dessert. Make the most of juicy peaches when they're in season with this guilt-free summer indulgence.

INGREDIENTS

1.25kg (2¾lb) ripe peaches,
    stoned and chopped
60g (2oz) sucralose
    sweetener (Splenda)
juice of 1 lemon

SERVES 4

 **PREP** 15 MINS,
PLUS FREEZING

1 Put the peaches in a food processor or blender and whizz until smooth. Pass through a sieve to make a smooth purée.

2 Tip the purée into a clean food processor or blender along with 180ml (6fl oz) water, the sweetener, and the lemon juice. Whizz again until smooth.

3 Pour the mixture into a freezerproof container with a lid, and put it in the freezer for 1–2 hours until it has almost set. Remove and stir well with a fork to break up the ice crystals, or put back in the food processor and whizz again. Return to the freezer for 4–5 hours until frozen. Serve scoops of sorbet in individual glass dishes.

Cook's tip: Choose a shallow container if you can, as the sorbet will freeze more quickly.

Nutrition data per serving

Energy	83kcals/355kJ
Carbohydrate	19g
of which sugar	18g
Fat	0g
of which saturates	0g
Salt	trace
Fibre	4g

Carpaccio of oranges with pistachio nuts

A deliciously refreshing, Moroccan-inspired dessert that is low in calories but full of flavour.

INGREDIENTS

4 oranges
2 pomegranates
generous pinch ground cinnamon
30g (1oz) shelled pistachio nuts,
 roughly chopped

SERVES 4

PREP 10 MINS, PLUS CHILLING

1 Using a sharp knife, remove the skin and pith from the oranges and slice the flesh into rounds. Sprinkle with the cinnamon and chill for 15 minutes.

2 Remove the seeds from the pomegranates, and discard the white membrane.

3 Place the orange slices on a serving dish, and sprinkle with the pomegranate seeds and pistachio nuts.

Nutrition data per serving

Energy	125kcals/525kJ
Carbohydrate	18g
of which sugar	18g
Fat	4g
of which saturates	0.5g
Salt	0.1g
Fibre	4g

Angel food cake

This American classic is named for its pure white, light-as-air fat-free sponge. It is best eaten on the day it is made.

INGREDIENTS

large knob of butter,
for greasing

150g (5½oz) plain flour, sifted

100g (3½oz) icing sugar, sifted,
plus extra for dusting

8 egg whites (keep the yolks
for custards and tart fillings)

pinch of cream of tartar

250g (9oz) caster sugar

few drops of almond or
vanilla extract

For the frosting

150g (5½oz) caster sugar

2 egg whites

strawberries (halved),
blueberries, and raspberries,
to decorate

SERVES 8-12　　**PREP 30 MINS**　　**COOK 35-45 MINS**

1 Preheat the oven to 180°C (350°F/Gas 4). Melt the butter in a small pan and use generously to brush the inside of a 1.7-litre (3-pint) ring mould. Sift the flour and icing sugar, again, into a bowl.

2 Whisk the egg whites and cream of tartar until stiff, then whisk in the caster sugar, 1 tbsp at a time. Sift the flour mixture into the egg white mixture and fold it in with a metal spoon, then fold in the almond or vanilla extract.

3 Spoon the mixture gently into the ring mould, filling right to the brim, and level the surface with a palette knife. Place the mould on a baking tray and bake for 35–45 minutes, or until just firm to the touch.

4 Carefully remove the cake from the oven and invert the mould onto a wire rack. Leave the cake to cool, then ease it out of the mould.

5 To make the frosting, place the caster sugar in a saucepan with 4 tbsp of water. Heat gently, stirring, until the sugar dissolves. Now increase the heat and boil until the syrup reaches "soft-ball" stage (114–118°C/238–245°F) on a sugar thermometer, or until a little of the syrup forms a soft ball when dropped into very cold water.

6 Meanwhile, whisk the egg whites until stiff. As soon as the sugar syrup reaches the correct temperature, plunge the base of the pan into a sink of cold water to stop the syrup getting any hotter. Pour the syrup into the egg whites, whisking constantly, in a slow, steady stream into the centre of the bowl. Keep whisking for 5 minutes, or until stiff peaks form.

7 Working quickly, because the frosting will set, spread it thinly all over the inside and outside of the cake with a palette knife, swirling the surface to create texture. Top with strawberries, blueberries, and raspberries, and sift over icing sugar to serve.

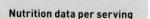

Nutrition data per serving

Energy	299kcals/1273kJ
Carbohydrate	70g
of which sugar	62g
Fat	0.2g
of which saturates	0g
Salt	0.1g
Fibre	0.5g

Brown bread autumn fruit pudding

For a seasonal twist on the more usual summer pudding, try this nourishing version with brown bread, gently poached autumn fruit, and a hint of cinnamon.

INGREDIENTS

6 tbsp apple juice

2 tbsp soft, light brown sugar

¼ tsp cinnamon

2–3 apples, about 200g (7oz) in total, peeled, cored, and cut into 1cm (½in) cubes

1 large pear, about 125g (4½oz) in total, peeled, cored and cut into 1cm (½in) cubes

150g (5½oz) blackberries, cut in half if large

7–8 thick slices good-quality day old brown bread, crusts removed

SERVES 4

PREP 30 MINS, PLUS CHILLING

COOK 15 MINS

1 Heat the apple juice, brown sugar, and cinnamon in a medium-sized, heavy-based saucepan. Add the apples and pear and cook, covered, over a low heat for 5 minutes, until they start to soften. Add the blackberries and cook for a further 5 minutes, until the fruit is soft. Strain the fruit through a sieve, reserving the juice in a shallow dish.

2 Line a 1 litre (2 pint) pudding bowl with cling film, leaving at least a 10cm (4in) overhang on all sides. Take each slice of bread and briefly dip one side into the juice. Use the bread, dipped-side down, to line the bowl. Press it firmly to fit the shape of the bowl, making sure the slices overlap slightly and there are no gaps. Leave 2 slices for the lid.

3 Pour the fruit into the bread-lined bowl. Then pour over most of the leftover juice, reserving a little for the top. Use the final two slices of bread to make a lid for the fruit, making sure it is well sealed. Patch up any gaps with small pieces of bread, if needed. Brush the top with the reserved juice.

4 Fold the overhanging cling film over the top of the pudding. Place a small plate or saucer on top of the pudding and weigh it down with heavy cans. Place the weighted pudding in the fridge overnight to set.

5 To serve the pudding, peel back the cling film from the top and place a serving plate on top of the bowl. Invert the bowl to turn the pudding out onto the plate and gently peel the cling film away from the pudding. Serve with Greek yogurt or whipped cream.

Nutrition data per serving

Energy	213 kcals/892kJ
Carbohydrate	44g
of which sugar	21g
Fat	2g
of which saturates	0.3g
Salt	0.8g
Fibre	8g

Low-fat ginger tea bread

This low-fat cake is quick and easy to make, and perfect
for an afternoon snack that won't pile on the calories.

INGREDIENTS

150g (5¹/₂oz) mixed dried fruit

325ml (11fl oz) lemon and
   ginger tea (made with
   2 tea bags)

225g (8oz) plain
   wholemeal flour

2 tsp baking powder

100g (3¹/₂oz) fructose

1 egg, beaten

MAKES 1 LOAF    **PREP** 15 MINS,
                          PLUS SOAKING

COOK 45 MINS –
1 HR

1 Place the dried fruit in a large heatproof bowl, pour the tea over
it and leave to stand for at least 2 hours, stirring occasionally.

2 Preheat the oven to 160°C (325°F/Gas 3). Grease and line the
bottom of a 900g (2lb) loaf tin with non-stick baking parchment.

3 Place the flour, baking powder, fructose, and egg in a food
processor or blender and process for a couple of minutes.
Add the dried fruit and tea and whizz again until well mixed.

4 Spoon the mixture into the prepared loaf tin, brush the surface
with a little water and bake for 45 minutes–1 hour until the cake
looks done and feels springy in the centre. You may need to cover it
with foil halfway through cooking if it is browning too quickly.

5 Allow the cake to cool in the tin for 5 minutes, then carefully
turn out on to a wire cooling rack.

Nutrition data per serving

Energy	106kcals/450kJ
Carbohydrate	23g
of which sugar	8g
Fat	0.8g
of which saturates	0.2g
Salt	0.2g
Fibre	1g

Acknowledgments

The Diabetes Cooking Book (2010) **Authors** Fiona Hunter and Heather Whinney; **Art director** Luis Peral; **Food stylist** Cara Hobday; **Prop stylist** Victoria Allen; **Home economists** Richard Harris, Emily Shardlow, and Rachel Wood; **Out-of-house editors** Helena Caldon and Fiona Corbridge; **Project editors** Robert Sharman and Saloni Talwar; **Designers** Katherine Raj and Devika Dwarkadas; **Senior creative art editor** Caroline de Souza.

The Gluten-Free Cookbook (2012) **Authors** Fiona Hunter, Jane Lawrie, and Heather Whinney; **Recipe editors** Jane Bamforth and Holly Kyte; **Recipe testers** Rebecca Blackstone, Anna Burges-Lumsden, Amy Carter, Jan Fullwood, Laura Fyfe, Katy Greenwood, Anne Harnan, Catherine Rose, and Rachel Wood; **Food stylists** Marie-Ange Lapierre and Emily Jonzen; **Hand model** Danaya Bunnag; **Senior editors** Alastair Laing and Chitra Subramanyam; **Project art editors** Katherine Raj, Prashant Kumar, and Anamica Roy.

Family Kitchen Cookbook (2013) **Author** Caroline Bretherton; **Nutritionist** Fiona Hunter; **New photography** Lis Parsons, William Reavell, and Stuart West; **Photography art direction** Susan Downing, Geoff Fennell, Lisa Pettibone, and Penny Stock; **Food styling** Emma-Jane Frost, Paul Jackman, Jane Lawrie, Rosie Reynolds, and Penny Stephens; **Prop styling** Susan Downing, Liz Hippisley, and Wei Tang; **Photography shoot manager** Anne Fisher; **Consultant for Babies and Toddlers chapter** Rosan Meyer; **Recipe testers** Jane Bamforth, Ramona Andrews, Anna Burges-Lumsden, Amy Carter, Sue Davie, Francesca Dennis, Hulya Erdal, Georgina Fuggle, Jan Fullwood, Anne Harnan, Richard Harris, Sue Harris, Jo Kerr, Sarah King, Emma Lahaye, Bren Parkins-Knight, Ann Reynolds, Cathy Seward, Rachel Wood, and Amanda Wright; **Senior editors** Scarlett O'Hara and Dorothy Kikon; **Senior art editors** Sara Robin and Ivy Roy; **Editors** Lucy Bannell.

Family Nutrition (2014) **Author** Jane Clarke; **Recipe consultant** Caroline Bretherton; **Nutritionist** Fiona Hunter; **Recipe tester** Katy Greenwood; **Prop stylist** Isabel de Cordova; **Food stylist** Jane Lawrie; **New photography** William Reavell; **Senior editors** Camilla Hallinan and Ira Sharma; **Project art editor** Katherine Raj and Simran Kaur; **Editors** Carolyn Humphries and Diana Vowles; **Designers** Mandy Earey, Saskia Janssen, and Simon Murrell.

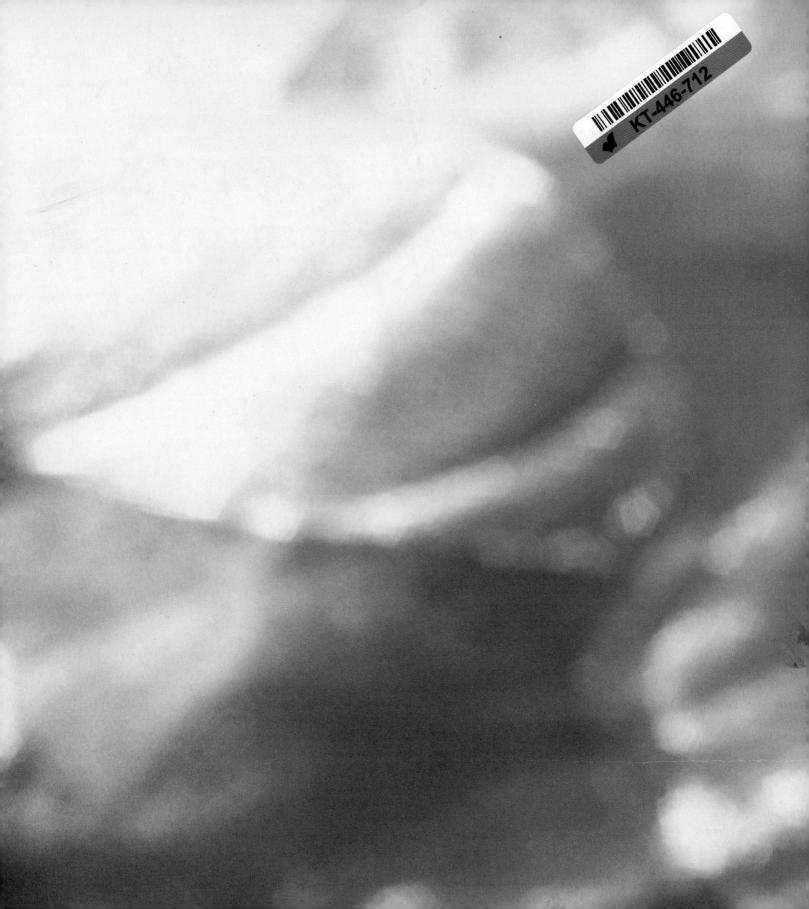

CURRY

CURRY

David Lee

hamlyn

First published in Great Britain in 1997
by Hamlyn, a division of Octopus Publishing Group Ltd
2–4 Heron Quays, London E14 4JP

This edition published 2002 by Octopus Publishing Group Ltd

Reprinted 2004

Copyright ©1997, 2002 Octopus Publishing Group Ltd

ISBN 0 600 61113 2

Printed in China

NOTES

Both metric and imperial measurements have been given in all
recipes. Use one set of measurements only and not a
mixture of both.

Standard level spoon measurements are used in all recipes.
1 tablespoon = one 15 ml spoon
1 teaspoon = one 5 ml spoon

Eggs should be medium to large unless otherwise stated.
The Department of Health advises that eggs should not be
consumed raw. This book contains dishes made with raw or
lightly cooked eggs. It is prudent for more vulnerable people,
such as pregnant and nursing mothers, invalids, the elderly,
babies and young children to avoid uncooked or lightly cooked
dishes made with eggs. Once prepared, these dishes should be
kept refrigerated and used promptly.

Milk should be full fat unless otherwise stated.

Meat and poultry should be cooked thoroughly. To test if poultry
is cooked, pierce the flesh through the thickest part with a
skewer or fork – the juices should run clear, never pink or red. Do
not re-freeze poultry that has been frozen previously and thawed.
Do not re-freeze a dish that has been frozen previously.

Pepper should be freshly ground black pepper unless
otherwise stated.

Fresh herbs should be used, unless otherwise stated. If
unavailable, use dried herbs as an alternative but halve the
quantities stated.

Measurements for canned food have been given as a standard
metric equivalent.

Nuts and nut derivatives
This book includes dishes made with nuts and nut derivatives. It
is advisable for customers with known allergic reactions to nuts
and nut derivatives and those who may be potentially vulnerable
to these allergies, such as pregnant and nursing mothers, invalids,
the elderly, babies and children, to avoid dishes made with nuts
and nut oils. It is also prudent to check the labels of pre-prepared
ingredients for the possible inclusion of nut derivatives.

Ovens should be preheated to the specified temperature – if
using a fan-assisted oven, follow the manufacturer's instructions
for adjusting the time and the temperature.

The heat and flavour of fresh, dried and ground chillies, curry
pastes and spices varies enormously, so always add small amounts
first, then taste and adjust the amounts as required.

Always take care when using chillies. After preparation, wash
your hands, knives and chopping board thoroughly and never let
any part of the chilli get near your eyes.

Preparing fresh chillies. For a very hot result, break off the stalk
and wash the chilli under cold running water. For a milder
flavour, remove the seeds: cut the chilli in half lengthways with a
sharp knife. Scrape out the seeds with the point of a knife and
cut away the fleshy white ribs from each half.

Contents

Introduction

'Curry' is an anglicized Indian word, derived, it is thought, either from *kari*, a Tamil word for sauce, or from *karhai*, a widely used Indian cooking vessel. Originally it meant food stewed with liquid and various spices and other flavourings, which cook together to form a sauce – an Oriental casserole, in fact. Now, 'curry' has taken on a wider meaning, signifying a generally hot, sometimes fiery dish, richly flavoured with spices and herbs.

Thus, in this book, there are recipes for soups and starters and for fish and shellfish dishes alongside the meat and poultry stews and vegetable dishes which are what we usually think of when we use the word 'curry'.

Not all curries come from India, as a glance at this book will show, for spiced dishes are popular in the cuisines of Thailand, Malaysia and Indonesia. Because both the Chinese and the Indians have had an influence on South-east Asian cooking, these curries tend to be less obviously 'Indian' and contain milder flavours as well as the hotter ones more often associated with curries.

In India itself there have been numerous outside influences on the country's cooking. The subtly spiced

curries from the north, especially Kashmir, owe much to the sophistication of the cooks at the luxurious courts of the Mughal emperors, who conquered northern India from Persia. The British, too, had an influence on Indian cooking: Mulligatawny Soup (see page 10) was invented to suit British Army demands for a soup course at dinner. Balti dishes are both Indian and British, for Balti is a type of Kashmiri curry from Baltistan, in Pakistan, which was developed in the Midlands of Britain by immigrants after the Second World War. Pakoras (the Indian vegetable fritters on pages 8 and 13) – an exotic nibble to serve with drinks before dinner – are a comparatively recent import to Britain.

SPICES IN CURRY COOKING

While there are numerous distinctly flavoured ingredients which recur frequently in curry making, such as coconut, ginger, onions and tamarind, no dish can be called a curry if it does not contain a selection of spices. Many spices are used in making curries, all of them with a distinctive flavour to offer – which is why there are so many curries in India, for there is almost no limit to the possible combinations of spices. Balti curries, served in their distinctive two-handled metal pan, are subtle rather than fiery, and simple to improvise, for they are based on ingredients found in most kitchens, such as onions, tomatoes, cumin and coriander.

It is best to keep only small quantities of frequently used spices in the kitchen, storing them in a cool, dry place and using them within six months, for a stale spice has little to offer any curry. An electric coffee grinder, kept specially for the purpose, makes grinding whole spices easy.

Among the most widely used spices in curry-making are:
ANISEED: small seeds with a liquorice flavour, widely used in India to flavour confectionery and chutneys.

ASAFOETIDA: pale yellow spice with a strong and distinctive flavour which helps enhance other flavours in a recipe, particularly in Indian bean and lentil dishes.

BLACK ONION SEEDS (Kalonji): small black seeds with an appealingly earthy flavour, used in Bengal in fish and vegetable dishes and in other parts of India in pickles.

CARDAMOM (pods and seeds): highly aromatic green pods widely used in Indian cookery. If they are used whole in a recipe, they should be removed before serving; the seeds (best removed from the pods as you need them, not bought in packets) are left in the dish.

CHILLIES (fresh red and green chillies; dried red chillies; also CAYENNE PEPPER): chillies, brought to India from Central America, give curries their fiery heat. If fresh or dried chillies are not available, cayenne pepper (called red chilli powder in Indian groceries) makes a good substitute. A chilli is less fiery if the seeds are removed from the pod. When handling chillies never touch your face or rub your eyes until you have washed your hands. Chilli paste and chilli sauce are also available.

CINNAMON: a spice from the bark of a small evergreen tree. This is used in Indian cookery, in savoury meat and rice dishes, and in sweets. It is used in the form of sticks, rather than as a powder. The sticks are used whole or in large pieces and should be removed from a dish before it is served.

CLOVES: a strongly aromatic spice used in Indian meat and rice dishes. Usually used whole, not ground, and removed from the dish before serving.

CORIANDER SEEDS: an essential and distinctive curry flavouring. The round, light brown seeds are used whole or ground in meat and vegetable dishes. Chopped coriander roots are used in Thai cooking, while fresh coriander leaves are popular in India as a flavouring for all kinds of curry.

CUMIN: these seeds, available in both black and white and also in ground form, are an important spice in Indian cooking.

FENNEL SEEDS: these have a mildly aniseed flavour and are used in meat and vegetable dishes.

FENUGREEK: seeds with a strong and bittersweet flavour, used sparingly in curry powders.

MUSTARD SEEDS: tiny, round seeds, usually described as black, though they are, in fact, reddish-brown. They take on a deliciously nutty flavour when scattered into hot oil at the beginning of a recipe.

NUTMEG: fragrant spice, best used freshly grated, for which special small nutmeg graters are obtainable.

SAFFRON (threads and powder): an expensive spice, used in dishes for special occasions both for its lovely yellow colour and its aroma.

TURMERIC: a spice with a mild, earthy flavour, widely used in Indian cooking to impart a good deep yellow colour.

DRY-FRYING SPICES

Dry-frying, or roasting, spices brings out their distinctive flavours. It is usual in Indian cooking to dry-fry several whole spices at once, depending on what will be needed in the recipe being prepared. Use a heavy-based frying pan and put all the spices in an even layer into the pan set over a moderate heat. Stir-fry the spices for about 5 minutes, until they are a shade or two darker and beginning to give off a delicious aroma. Allow the spices to cool, then grind them in a mortar or an electric coffee grinder.

SOME BASIC RECIPES

These recipes include basic mixtures and curry pastes used in a variety of dishes and two garnishes with the distinct flavour of Oriental cooking.

COCONUT MILK AND CREAM

Mix 400 g/13 oz grated or desiccated coconut with 900 ml/1½ pints milk in a saucepan, bring to the boil, lower the heat and simmer, stirring occasionally, until the mixture has reduced by one third. Strain, extracting as much liquid as possible. Pour the strained milk into a bowl and chill in the refrigerator. When it is cold, skim off the thicker 'cream' that rises to the surface. The remaining liquid is the coconut milk.

Coconut milk is particularly good with shellfish, as in the recipe for Siamese Pineapple and Mussel Curry (see page 20).

THAI RED CURRY PASTE

Deseed 6 dried red chillies and soak them in water for 10 minutes. Drain well and chop roughly. Place in a food processor and work to a smooth paste

MAKING PAKORAS (INDIAN VEGETABLE FRITTERS)

1 To make the fritter batter, the flour is sifted into a bowl, then salt and chilli powder are added and water or yogurt are beaten in. The batter is left to stand until it is very thick, before any herbs and spices are added.

2 The prepared vegetable pieces, such as onion rings, spinach, chopped courgettes and cooked sliced potatoes, are dipped into the batter and turned in it so that they are thoroughly coated. The oil for deep-frying is heated in a heavy saucepan or deep-fat fryer.

3 The pakoras are fried in the hot oil, a few at a time, until they are golden and crisp. When cooked, they are lifted out with a slotted spoon and dried on kitchen paper. Pakoras are best served warm, with a chutney or hot sauce.

with 2 tablespoons chopped lemon grass, 1 tablespoon chopped shallot, 1 tablespoon chopped garlic, 1 tablespoon chopped coriander stem, 1 teaspoon chopped galangal, 2 teaspoons coriander seeds, 1 teaspoon cumin seeds, 6 white peppercorns, 1 teaspoon cumin seeds, 1 teaspoon salt and 1 teaspoon shrimp paste. Store in a screwtop jar in the refrigerator for up to 3 weeks.

This curry paste is a splendid addition to recipes as diverse as Laksa (see page 12) and Thai Red Beef Curry (see page 55).

Garlic Mixture
Put 2 tablespoons crushed garlic, 2 tablespoons chopped coriander stem

and ½ teaspoon pepper into a mortar and pound to a paste. This pungent mixture gives an extra piquancy to fish dishes such as Thai Grilled Mullet (see page 16).

Thai Green Curry Paste
Remove the stems and seeds from 6 dried green chillies. Place them in a food processor and work to a smooth paste with 3 tablespoons finely chopped spring onions, 1 tablespoon chopped garlic, 1 tablespoon chopped lemon grass, 1 tablespoon shrimp paste, 1 teaspoon ground galangal (laos powder), 1 teaspoon caraway seeds, 2 teaspoons coriander seeds, 1 teaspoon finely grated lemon rind and 1 teaspoon salt. Green curry paste

can be stored in a screwtop jar in the refrigerator for up to 3 weeks.

This curry paste is an excellent base for recipes including poultry. In this book, it is used in Green Duck Curry (see page 28) and Thai Green Chicken Curry (see page 34). Although it is not as fiery as red curry paste, it is still a hot spice mixture.

Fried Onion Rings
Heat about 300 ml/½ pint vegetable oil in a wok or deep-fat fryer until hot but not smoking, add 1 large, thinly sliced onion and deep-fry for 3–4 minutes, until golden brown. Remove from the pan with a slotted spoon and drain on kitchen paper. Serve them hot or at room temperature. These Fried Onion

Rings make an eye-appealing garnish and are particularly good served with rice dishes, such as Pilau Rice (see page 90).

FRIED ONION FLAKES

Measure out 50 g/2 oz dried onion flakes. Heat about 300 ml/½ pint vegetable oil in a deep-fat fryer to 180–190°C/350–375°F. Put a quarter of the onion flakes in a metal sieve and lower them into the hot oil, frying them for a few seconds until they are golden brown. Remove from the fat and drain on kitchen paper. Repeat with the remaining onion flakes. Cool, then store in an airtight container. Onion flakes will keep for 3–4 weeks.

The dried onion flakes for this

Indonesian garnish are available from Asian grocers and most large supermarkets.

GARNISHING CURRIES

A crisply prepared, single-colour garnish is ideal for curries, which is why fresh herbs are among the most popular garnishes in Oriental cooking. One of the best garnish herbs is coriander, its broad, brightly green leaves standing out well against the colours and ingredients of most curries. Other often-used herbs are parsley (especially the flat-leafed variety), mint and Thai basil.

Chillies are used in various forms as garnishes. Small dried red chillies are often used whole as a garnish,

while fresh red chillies may be cut into a flower (for dishes in which the Chinese influence is strong) or sliced into rings. Chilli powder is also often used as a garnish.

Fruits and vegetables making good garnishes include lemons and limes (cut into slices or wedges), onions (thin slices served either raw or fried, as in Fried Onion Rings, on page 8) and spring onions (cut into rings for curries, rather than into the spring onion tassels used in Chinese cooking). Red and green peppers make a good garnish, too, usually served thinly sliced. Not a garnish as such, but essential accompaniments to curries, are chapati and other breads, chutneys and cooling raitas.

MAKING CHAPATI (UNLEAVENED BREAD)

1 The flour and salt are mixed with water to a soft, supple dough, which is kneaded for 10 minutes. It is then put in a bowl, covered and left to rise in a cool place for 30 minutes. The dough is knocked back and kneaded thoroughly and divided into 12 pieces.

2 Each piece of dough is put on a lightly floured surface and rolled out with a rolling pin into a thin round pancake.

3 A griddle or heavy frying pan is lightly greased and set over a moderate heat. The chapatis are cooked, one at a time, being pressed down with a fish slice. When blisters appear on the chapati it is turned over and cooked on the other side until lightly coloured. They are served warm, brushed with a little butter and folded into quarters.

Soups and Starters

Mulligatawny Soup

Mulligatawny has no history in India before the British Raj – this spicy soup was simply an invention to satisfy the demands of army officers for a soup course at dinner. The literal translation of the Tamil word 'mulligatawny' is pepper water.

50 g/2 oz dried tamarind

1.2 litres/2 pints beef stock

50 g/2 oz ghee or butter

1 large onion, sliced

2 garlic cloves, sliced

1 teaspoon ground ginger

2 teaspoons pepper

2 teaspoons ground coriander

½ teaspoon ground fenugreek

½ teaspoon chilli powder

1½ teaspoons turmeric

1½ teaspoons salt

thinly sliced red and green

peppers, to garnish

1 Put the dried tamarind into a saucepan, add just enough of the beef stock to cover, then bring to the boil. Remove the pan from the heat, cover and leave the tamarind to soak for 4 hours.

2 Melt the ghee or butter in a wok or heavy-based saucepan, add the onion and garlic and fry gently for about 4–5 minutes until soft.

3 Add the ginger, pepper, ground coriander, fenugreek, chilli powder, turmeric and salt and fry for 3 minutes, stirring constantly. Stir in the remaining beef stock. Strain the tamarind liquid through a wire sieve over a small bowl, pressing to extract as much liquid as possible. Add the tamarind juice to the wok and simmer for 15 minutes. Taste and adjust the seasoning before serving, garnished with the sliced peppers. Serve hot.

Serves 4

Preparation time: 10 minutes, plus soaking

Cooking time: 25 minutes

Laksa

The English translation of this Malaysian dish is Rice Noodles with Curried Chicken Soup. Despite its name, it really is a meal in itself.

- 6 tablespoons vegetable oil
- 250 g/8 oz pressed beancurd, cubed
- 2 red onions, finely chopped
- 3 garlic cloves, finely chopped
- 4 Brazil nuts, finely grated
- 2 teaspoons ground cumin
- 1 tablespoon ground coriander
- ½ teaspoon turmeric
- 1 red chilli, deseeded and chopped
- 1 green chilli, deseeded and chopped
- ½ teaspoon shrimp paste
- 2 tablespoons Thai red curry paste (see pages 7–8)
- 1 litre/1¾ pints coconut milk (see page 7)
- 1 tablespoon soft brown sugar
- 375 g/12 oz cooked chicken breasts, shredded
- 125 g/4 oz bean sprouts
- 1 tablespoon chopped fresh coriander
- 250 g/8 oz dried rice vermicelli or noodles
- salt and pepper

TO GARNISH:
- 2 fresh red chillies, chopped
- fresh coriander leaves
- 3 spring onions, sliced

1 Heat 2 tablespoons of the oil in a wok. Fry the beancurd in the oil, in 2 batches, turning it frequently. Cook each batch for 5 minutes until crisp and golden, then remove with a slotted spoon, place to drain on kitchen paper and set aside.

2 Heat 2 more tablespoons of oil in the wok, add the onion and garlic and fry over a gentle heat, stirring frequently, for 5 minutes until softened.
3 Add the Brazil nuts, the ground cumin, coriander and turmeric, the red and green chillies and the shrimp and curry pastes to the wok. Stir well to mix and fry for a further 2 minutes.
4 Stir in the coconut milk and sugar and season generously with salt and pepper. Bring the curried coconut milk to the boil, then reduce the heat and simmer gently for 6 minutes. Taste and adjust the seasoning if necessary.
5 Heat the remaining oil in a frying pan, add the chicken and stir-fry for 6 minutes until golden. Add the bean sprouts and chopped coriander and stir-fry for a further 1 minute.
6 Place the vermicelli or noodles in a bowl and pour boiling water over them to cover completely. Allow to stand for 5 minutes, then drain well.
7 To serve, divide the vermicelli among 4 soup bowls. Place a quarter of the fried beancurd and a quarter of the chicken and bean sprout mixture on top of each portion of noodles. Ladle over the hot curry sauce and scatter over the suggested garnishes. Serve immediately.

Serves 4
Preparation time: about 20 minutes
Cooking time: 40 minutes

Pakoras

These spicy nibbles, from northern India, can be served as a starter or with drinks. Discard the seeds from the chillies for a less spicy version.

- 125 g/4 oz gram or chickpea flour
- 1 teaspoon salt
- ½ teaspoon chilli powder
- about 150 ml/¼ pint water or yogurt
- 2 green chillies, finely chopped
- 1 tablespoon finely chopped fresh coriander
- 1 teaspoon melted butter or ghee
- 2 onions, cut into rings
- oil, for deep-frying
- 8 small fresh spinach leaves
- 2–3 potatoes, parboiled and sliced

1 Sift the flour, salt and chilli powder into a bowl. Stir in sufficient water or yogurt to make a thick batter and beat well until smooth. Cover the bowl and leave to stand for 30 minutes.

2 Stir the chillies and coriander into the batter, then add the melted butter or ghee. Drop in the onion rings to coat thickly with batter.

3 Heat the oil in a deep pan, add the onion rings and deep-fry until crisp and golden. Remove from the pan with a slotted spoon, drain on kitchen paper and keep warm.

4 Dip the spinach leaves into the batter and deep-fry in the same way, adding more oil to the pan if necessary.

5 Finally, repeat the process with the potato slices. Serve hot, with a chilli sauce, if liked.

Serves 4

Preparation time: 15–20 minutes, plus standing

Cooking time: about 25 minutes

Prawn and Egg Sambal

- 500 g/1 lb tiger prawn tails
- 4 hard-boiled eggs, shelled and quartered
- 300 ml/½ pint coconut milk (see page 7)
- 1 small onion, finely chopped
- 1 garlic clove, crushed
- 1 fresh green chilli, deseeded and chopped
- juice of ½ lemon
- pinch of chilli powder
- ½ teaspoon salt

TO GARNISH:
- 50 g/2 oz cooked green peas
- chopped fresh coriander leaves

1 Arrange the prawns and eggs in a shallow serving dish, then cover and chill in the refrigerator while you make the sauce.
2 Place the coconut milk, onion, garlic, chilli, lemon juice, chilli powder and salt in a food processor and purée until smooth and evenly mixed. Pour the mixture over the prawns and eggs, then cover and chill until required.
3 Serve the sambal well chilled, garnished with the peas and chopped fresh coriander, and accompanied by poppadoms if you like.

Serves 4
Preparation time: 15 minutes, plus chilling

Vegetable Samosas

PASTRY:

- 125 g/4 oz plain flour
- ¼ teaspoon salt
- 25 g/1 oz ghee or butter
- 2–3 tablespoons water

FILLING:

- 1 tablespoon oil
- 1 teaspoon mustard seeds
- 1 small onion, finely chopped
- 2 green chillies, minced
- ¼ teaspoon turmeric
- 1 teaspoon finely chopped fresh root ginger
- salt
- 125 g/4 oz frozen peas
- 125 g/4 oz cooked potatoes, diced
- ½ tablespoon chopped fresh coriander
- 1 tablespoon lemon juice
- oil, for deep-frying

1 First make the pastry. Sift the flour and salt into a bowl. Rub in the ghee or butter until the mixture resembles breadcrumbs. Add the water and knead to a very smooth dough. Cover and chill while preparing the filling.

2 Heat the oil in a large saucepan and add the mustard seeds. Leave for a few seconds until they start to pop, then add the onion and fry for about 5 minutes until golden.

3 Add the chillies, turmeric, ginger and salt to taste and fry for 3 minutes; if the mixture starts sticking add ½ tablespoon water and stir well. Add the peas, stir well and cook for 2 minutes. Add the potatoes and coriander, stir well and cook for 1 minute. Stir in the lemon juice. Cool slightly.

4 Divide the pastry into 8 pieces. Dust with flour and roll each piece into a thin round, then cut each round in half. Fold each half into a cone and brush the seam with water to seal.

5 Fill the cone with a spoonful of filling (do not overfill), dampen the top edge and seal firmly. Heat the oil and deep-fry the samosas until crisp and golden. Serve hot or warm with a raita.

Serves 4

Preparation time: 15 minutes, plus chilling

Cooking time: about 30 minutes

Fish and Shellfish

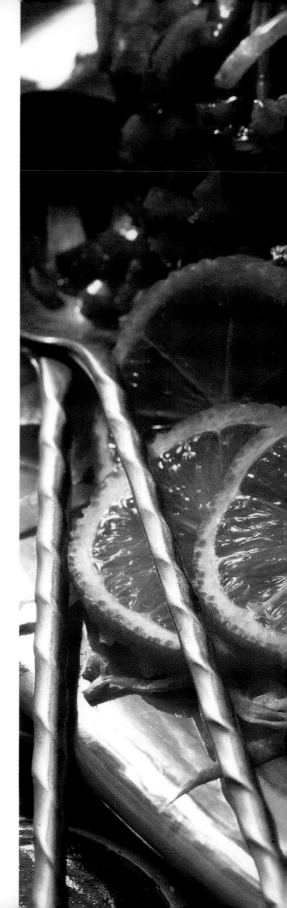

Thai Grilled Mullet

1 medium grey mullet, cleaned

½ tablespoon garlic mixture (see page 8)

½ onion, chopped

5 mushrooms, wiped and sliced

2 tablespoons shredded root ginger

1 celery stick, sliced

1 teaspoon pepper

1 tablespoon tao chiew (salted soya bean flavouring)

1 tablespoon oyster sauce

250 ml/8 fl oz fish stock or water

TO SERVE:

1 lettuce, separated into leaves

3 lemon slices

1 Place the fish on a wooden board and score the skin 2–3 times with a sharp knife to allow the sauce to be absorbed during cooking. Rub the fish with garlic mixture, pressing it well into the cuts. Transfer the fish to a shallow heatproof dish.

2 In a bowl, mix all the remaining ingredients well and pour over the fish. Place the fish under a preheated grill and cook for 20 minutes, turning the fish over halfway through the cooking time.

3 Just before serving, arrange a bed of lettuce on a shallow serving dish. Carefully transfer the fish to the dish, pour over the vegetable sauce and garnish with the lemon slices. Serve immediately.

Serves 4

Preparation time: 10–15 minutes

Cooking time: 20 minutes

Chilli Prawns with Cherry Tomatoes

Raw tiger prawn tails are available at good fishmongers and the fresh fish counters of large supermarkets. They are expensive but well worth it, for they are large, juicy, and full of flavour – far superior to the ubiquitous pale pink cooked variety.

- 3 tablespoons vegetable oil
- 1 small onion, finely chopped
- 2.5 cm/1 inch piece of fresh root ginger, peeled and finely chopped
- 2 garlic cloves, crushed
- 1–2 fresh chillies or 1–2 teaspoons chilli powder, according to taste
- 375 g/12 oz raw tiger prawn tails, defrosted and dried thoroughly if frozen, peeled
- 6–8 cherry tomatoes, halved
- 2 tablespoons tomato purée
- 1 tablespoon red or white wine vinegar
- pinch of caster sugar
- ½ teaspoon salt
- sprigs of coriander, to garnish

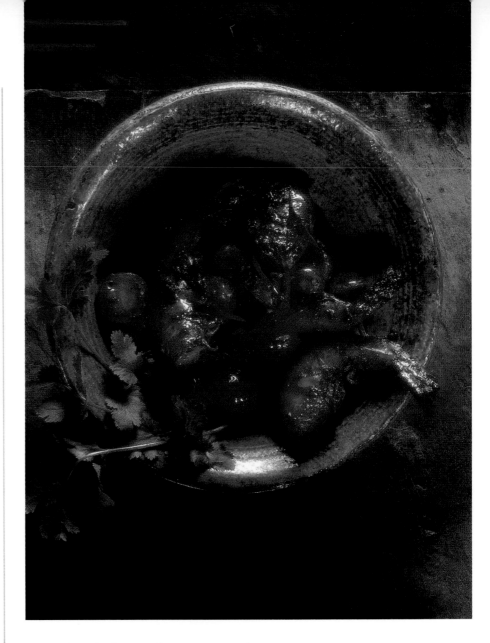

1 Heat a wok until hot. Add the oil and heat over moderate heat until hot. Add the onion, ginger, garlic and chillies or chilli powder and stir-fry for 2–3 minutes or until softened, taking care not to let the ingredients brown.

2 Add the prawns, increase the heat to high and stir-fry for 1–2 minutes or until they turn pink. Add the tomatoes, tomato purée, wine vinegar, sugar and salt. Increase the heat to high and stir-fry for several minutes or until the mixture is thick, taking care not to let the cherry tomatoes lose their shape. Taste and add more salt if necessary. Serve at once, garnished with sprigs of coriander.

Serves 4
Preparation time: 10 minutes
Cooking time: 10–15 minutes

Prawn Chilli Fry

This is a quick and easy way to transform a packet of cooked peeled prawns from the supermarket into a quick and delicious spicy supper dish. It has a less subtle flavour than Chilli Prawns with Cherry Tomatoes on page 18, but costs considerably less.

- **3 tablespoons oil**
- **3 onions, sliced**
- **2 green chillies, chopped**
- **2.5 cm/1 inch piece of fresh root ginger, chopped**
- **½ teaspoon chilli powder**
- **½ teaspoon turmeric**
- **salt**
- **375 g/12 oz cooked peeled prawns**

1 Heat the oil in a large frying pan, add the onions and fry gently for 5 minutes until soft and golden. Add the chillies, ginger, chilli powder, turmeric and salt to taste and fry for 2 minutes.
2 Add the prawns and cook, uncovered, for about 3 minutes or until all the moisture has evaporated. Serve immediately with boiled or fried rice.

Serves 4
Preparation time: 5 minutes
Cooking time: about 10 minutes

Siamese Pineapple and Mussel Curry

Sometimes known as holy basil, Thai basil is an Asian variety of popular European herb sweet basil. It has small green leaves and purple stems and flowers, and its flavour is a mixture of sweet basil and aniseed. It is found in Thai and Chinese shops, but sweet basil can be substituted if it is not available. Galangal is a spice popular in South-East Asia which looks, and tastes, rather like ginger.

- 1 kg/2 lb fresh mussels
- 2 stalks of lemon grass, roughly chopped
- 20 Thai basil leaves
- 2 tablespoons groundnut oil
- 2 tablespoons Thai red curry paste (see page 7)
- 5 cm/2 inch piece of fresh galangal, finely chopped
- 1 large green chilli, thinly sliced
- kaffir lime leaves, finely chopped
- 200 ml/7 fl oz coconut milk (see page 7)
- 1 tablespoon Thai fish sauce (nam pla)
- 1 teaspoon palm sugar or soft brown sugar
- 175 g/6 oz peeled fresh pineapple, cut into bite-sized pieces
- sprigs of Thai basil, to garnish (optional)

1 Scrub the mussels with a stiff brush and scrape off the beards and barnacles with a sharp knife. Wash well in cold water and discard any open mussels.

2 Pour about 2.5 cm/1 inch water into a large saucepan, add the chopped lemon grass and Thai basil and bring the water to the boil. Tip in the mussels, cover the pan and steam the mussels for 3–4 minutes or until they have opened and are cooked. Drain the mussels, discarding the lemon grass, Thai basil and any mussels which have not opened. Set the mussels on one side while preparing the sauce.

3 Heat the oil in a heavy-based saucepan, add the curry paste, galangal, chilli and lime leaves and fry over gentle heat, stirring, for about 4 minutes until fragrant. Stir in the coconut milk, fish sauce and sugar and cook for 1 further minute.

4 Reserve a few mussels in their shells for garnish and remove the remaining mussels from their shells. Add the shelled mussels and pineapple to the curry sauce. Stir gently and cook for 2–3 minutes to heat through. Serve hot, garnished with the reserved mussels and Thai basil, if using.

Serves 4
Preparation time: 30 minutes
Cooking time: 10–15 minutes

Fish Fillets in Spicy Turmeric and Coconut Sauce

- 4 thick haddock fillets (taken from the centre of the fish), skinned
- juice of 2 limes
- 2 teaspoons turmeric
- 1 small onion, roughly chopped
- 1–2 garlic cloves, roughly chopped
- 2 fresh chillies, deseeded and roughly chopped
- 2 teaspoons ground coriander
- 1 teaspoon ground galangal (laos powder)
- about 300 ml/½ pint vegetable oil, for shallow-frying
- 100 g/3½ oz creamed coconut, roughly chopped
- 1 teaspoon soft brown sugar
- ½ teaspoon salt

TO GARNISH:
- lime wedges
- chopped red chillies

1 Arrange the haddock fillets in a single layer in a shallow dish. Pour over the lime juice, then rub the turmeric into the flesh. Cover and leave to stand for about 20 minutes.

2 Meanwhile, place the onion, garlic, chillies, coriander and ground galangal in a food processor or blender and work to a paste, adding a little water if necessary. Set aside.

3 Heat the oil in a wok over moderate heat until hot but not smoking. With a fish slice, lower 2 of the haddock fillets into the hot oil and shallow-fry for 5 minutes, taking care to keep them whole. Remove with the fish slice and drain on kitchen paper. Shallow-fry and drain the 2 remaining fillets in the same way.

4 Pour off all but 2 tablespoons oil from the wok. Add the spice paste and stir-fry over a gentle heat for 3–4 minutes. Add the chopped coconut, then pour in 300 ml/½ pint boiling water and stir constantly until the coconut is dissolved. Add the sugar and salt and bring to the boil, stirring, then lower the heat and simmer until thickened, stirring frequently.

5 Return the haddock fillets to the wok and carefully spoon over the sauce, taking care not to break the pieces of fish. Heat through very gently, then transfer to warmed plates with a fish slice. Spoon the coconut sauce over and around the fish and garnish with lime wedges and chopped red chillies. Serve at once.

Serves 4
Preparation time: 10 minutes, plus standing
Cooking time: 25–30 minutes

Steamed Tuna Fish Curry in Banana Leaves

This is a fresh-tasting curry from southern India. It looks most attractive served on banana leaves, which can be bought at ethnic markets. If they are not available, wrap the tuna steaks in a double thickness of buttered greaseproof paper for steaming.

- 4 x 150 g/5 oz fresh tuna steaks
- juice of 1 lime
- 4 large pieces of banana leaf

GREEN CURRY PASTE:
- 1 tablespoon cumin seeds
- 2 tablespoons coriander seeds
- 3 large green chillies, deseeded and chopped
- 25 g/1 oz fresh mint leaves
- 5 cm/2 inch piece of fresh root ginger, grated
- 4 garlic cloves, crushed
- 25 g/1 oz caster sugar
- ½ teaspoon salt
- 75 g/3 oz desiccated coconut
- 50 ml/2 fl oz malt vinegar

TO GARNISH:
- 1 onion, cut into rings
- 2 green chillies, deseeded and cut into rings
- sprigs of mint
- lime wedges

1 Place the tuna steaks in a shallow, non-metallic dish and pour over the lime juice. Cover and set aside to marinate while making the curry paste.

2 To make the green curry paste, place the cumin and coriander seeds in a food processor or blender and process briefly. Add the chillies, mint, ginger and garlic, and work for 1 minute to produce a paste. Add the sugar, salt, coconut and vinegar, and blend again until all the ingredients are thoroughly combined.

3 Lay the pieces of banana leaf or buttered greaseproof paper on a flat surface. Remove the tuna from the lime juice and place a steak in the centre of each banana leaf. Spread the green curry paste over the tuna, completely covering the fish. Wrap up the banana leaves to enclose the pieces of fish, and fasten securely with wooden cocktail sticks.

4 Steam the fish over boiling water for 18–20 minutes, or until the fish flakes when tested with the point of a knife.

5 Garnish the fish with onion, chilli rings and mint springs, and serve with wedges of lime.

Serves 4
Preparation time: about 10 minutes
Cooking time: 20 minutes

Fish with Ginger and Soya

- 2 medium grey mullet or mackerel, cleaned
- oil, for deep-frying
- 2 tablespoons vegetable oil
- 2 garlic cloves, crushed
- 2 tablespoons shredded root ginger
- 1 tablespoon tao chiew (salted soya bean flavouring)
- 1 tablespoon sugar
- 1 teaspoon Thai fish sauce (nam pla)
- ½ teaspoon pepper
- 250 ml/8 fl oz fish stock or water
- 5 spring onions, sliced

TO GARNISH:
- fresh coriander leaves
- strips of red chilli

1 Cut the fish into large chunks and dry on kitchen paper. Heat the oil in a wok or deep-fat fryer and deep-fry the fish for 10–15 minutes until golden brown. Remove the fish with a slotted spoon and drain on kitchen paper.

2 Heat the vegetable oil in a saucepan large enough to hold the fish chunks in a single layer. Stir in the garlic and cook until pale gold in colour. Add the ginger, tao chiew, sugar, fish sauce and pepper and stir well.

3 Stir in the stock and bring the liquid to the boil. Add the fried fish and spring onions, lower the heat and simmer for 10 minutes.

4 Serve hot, garnished with coriander leaves and strips of red chilli.

Serves 4

Preparation time: 10 minutes
Cooking time: about 30 minutes

Fish Curry with Coconut Milk

The Indian name for this curry from southern India is Fish Molee.

- 750 g/1½ lb cod fillet, skinned
- 2 tablespoons plain flour
- 4 tablespoons oil
- 2 onions, sliced
- 2 garlic cloves, crushed
- 1 teaspoon turmeric
- 4 green chillies, deseeded and finely chopped
- 2 tablespoons lemon juice
- 175 ml/6 fl oz thick coconut milk (see page 7)
- salt

TO GARNISH:

- slices of red chilli
- snipped chives

1 Cut the fish into 4 and coat with the flour. Heat the oil in a frying pan, and fry the fish quickly on both sides. Lift out with a slotted spoon and set aside.
2 Add the onion and garlic to the pan and fry for about 5 minutes until soft and golden. Add the turmeric, chillies, lemon juice, coconut milk and salt to taste and simmer, uncovered, for 10 minutes or until thickened.
3 Add the fish and any juices, spoon over the sauce and cook gently for 2–3 minutes, until tender. Garnish with chillies and chives and serve at once.

Serves 4
Preparation time: 10 minutes
Cooking time: about 20 minutes

Assam Fish Curry

Assam means sour in Malay and usually implies that tamarind pulp is used in the cooking, for its distinctive, tangy flavour.

- 4 tablespoons vegetable oil
- 3 tablespoons tamarind pulp, soaked in 250 ml/8 fl oz boiling water for 10 minutes
- 2 tomatoes, quartered
- 2 baby aubergines, weighing about 50 g/ 2 oz each, quartered
- 2 large fresh red chillies, quartered lengthways and deseeded
- 1 tablespoon soft brown sugar
- ½ teaspoon salt
- 625 g/1¼ lb skinless haddock or halibut, cut into 5 cm/2 inch pieces

SPICE PASTE:

- 5 small dried chillies soaked in cold water for 10 minutes, then deseeded and chopped
- 8 shallots, chopped
- 3 stalks of lemon grass, chopped
- 2 fresh red chillies, deseeded and chopped
- 2.5 cm/1 inch piece of fresh galangal, chopped
- 2 teaspoon dried shrimp paste
- 1 teaspoon turmeric
- 5 candlenuts or macadamia nuts (optional)

1 To make the spice paste, put the dried chillies, shallots, lemon grass, red chillies, galangal, shrimp paste, turmeric and candlenuts or macadamia nuts, if using, in a food processor or blender and work to a thick paste. Heat the oil in a large saucepan, add the spice paste and fry over gentle heat, stirring constantly, for about 5 minutes until softened.

2 Strain the tamarind pulp through a sieve, pressing it against the sieve to extract as much tamarind flavour as possible. Discard the pulp and add the strained tamarind liquid to the pan with the tomatoes, aubergines and chillies. Bring to the boil, then reduce the heat, cover the pan and simmer gently for 12 minutes.

3 Add the sugar, salt and prepared fish to the pan and stir gently to coat the fish in the sauce. Cover the pan and cook the curry over a gentle heat for a further 7 minutes or until the fish is cooked through. Taste and adjust the seasoning if necessary. Serve the curry hot with plain boiled rice.

Serves 4

Preparation time: about 20 minutes, plus soaking
Cooking time: 25–30 minutes

VARIATION

Assam Squid Curry

Use the same ingredients as in the main recipe but replacing the fish with 375 g/12 oz small squid, cleaned but left whole. Follow the method in the main recipe until the final step when the squid is added to the pan. Cook the squid for about 5 minutes, stirring occasionally, leaving the pan uncovered at this stage.

Spicy Fried Fishcakes

- 500 g/1 lb cod fillet, skinned and cut into chunks
- 3 tablespoons Thai red curry paste (see page 7)
- 1 egg
- 3 tablespoons Thai fish sauce (nam pla)
- 75 g/3 oz French beans, finely chopped
- 1 tablespoon finely shredded makrut (citrus) leaves
- oil, for shallow frying

1 Combine the fish and the curry paste in a food processor or blender, and process until the fish is finely chopped. Alternatively, use a pestle and mortar.

2 Transfer the fish mixture to a bowl and add the egg and nam pla. Knead to make a stiff mixture. Work in the French beans and makrut leaves in the same way.

3 Form the mixture into 16–20 balls and flatten each one to a round about 1 cm/½ inch thick. Heat the oil in a large frying pan, add the fishcakes and fry for 4–5 minutes on each side over medium heat. Do not allow the fishcakes to overcook, or they will dry out.

4 Lift the fishcakes out of the pan with a slotted spoon and drain on kitchen paper, transfer to a serving plate and serve hot with a salad.

Serves 4

Preparation time: 15 minutes
Cooking time: about 10 minutes

Chicken and Duck

Green Duck Curry

2–2.5 kg/4–5 lb duckling with giblets
coarse salt, for sprinkling
500 ml/17 fl oz thick coconut milk (see page 7)
500 ml/17 fl oz thin coconut milk (see page 7)
4 kaffir lime leaves, more for garnish

2½ tablespoons Thai green curry paste (see page 8)
2–3 fresh green chillies, deseeded and sliced
Thai fish sauce (nam pla), to taste
sliced red chillies, to garnish

1 Dry the duck thoroughly with kitchen paper. Sprinkle the skin generously with coarse salt. Set aside for 15 minutes.

2 Brush off the salt and chop the duck into 5 cm/2 inch pieces. Heat a wok or frying pan over medium-high heat. Add a few pieces of duck and brown them thoroughly. Remove with a slotted spoon and drain on kitchen paper. Brown the remaining duck pieces in the same way. Discard the rendered fat from the wok and wipe it clean.

3 Reduce the heat to moderate. Skim the coconut cream from the top of the thick coconut milk and bring to the boil in the wok, then add the lime leaves and curry paste. Reduce the heat and cook, stirring constantly, until the oil begins to separate. Add the duck pieces, turn to cover evenly with the sauce then cook gently for 5 minutes.

4 Add the thick and thin coconut milks, bring just to the boil, then reduce the heat to very low. Simmer, stirring occasionally, for about 1–1¼ hours until the duck is tender.

5 Remove from the heat, transfer to a bowl and allow to cool. Cover and chill overnight.

6 Skin the excess fat from the curry, then return to the wok, stir in the chillies and season with Thai fish sauce. Simmer for 5 minutes or until heated through, then transfer to a warmed serving dish, garnish with sliced red chillies and shredded lime leaves and serve immediately.

Serves 4–6
Preparation time: 15 minutes, plus standing and chilling
Cooking time: 1½–1¾ hours

Oriental Chicken with Turmeric

Macadamia nuts are noted for their rich flavour and waxy texture. Be sure to buy the unsalted ones for this recipe. Serai or sereh powder is dried lemon grass, a convenient way of adding this lovely citrus flavour to Oriental curries and stir-fries. If you are lucky enough to be able to get fresh lemon grass, you can use it instead of the serai powder and lemon rind in this dish. You will need 1 stalk of lemon grass, bruised.

- 100 g/3½ oz creamed coconut, roughly chopped
- 50 g/2 oz macadamia nuts, roughly chopped
- 1 garlic clove, roughly chopped
- 3 tablespoons vegetable oil
- 1 onion, finely chopped
- 8 boneless chicken thighs, skinned and cut into large chunks
- 1 tablespoon turmeric
- 1 teaspoon serai powder
- thinly pared rind and juice of 1 lemon
- salt and pepper
- flat leaf parsley, to garnish

1 First make the coconut milk. Put the chopped coconut into a measuring jug, pour in boiling water up to the 300 ml/½ pint mark and stir until the coconut is dissolved. Set aside.
2 Pound half of the macadamia nuts to a paste with the garlic using a pestle and mortar. Heat a wok until hot. Add the oil and heat over moderate heat until hot. Add the onion together with the nut and garlic paste and stir-fry for 2–3 minutes or until the onion is softened, taking care not to let the ingredients brown.
3 Add the chicken pieces, increase the heat to high and stir-fry for 1–2 minutes or until the chicken is lightly coloured on all sides. Stir in the turmeric and serai powder and season to taste with salt and pepper. Add the coconut milk and bring to the boil, stirring constantly.

4 Lower the heat, add the lemon rind and juice and simmer for about 10 minutes or until the chicken is tender and the sauce thickened, stirring frequently to prevent sticking. Remove and discard the lemon rind. Taste the sauce for seasoning and serve hot, sprinkled with the remaining chopped macadamia nuts, and sprigs of flat leaf parsley .

Serves 3–4
Preparation time: 15 minutes
Cooking time: about 20 minutes

Burmese Chicken Curry and Cellophane Noodles

This traditional Burmese dish is served with noodles. It is the ideal dish for an informal dinner party, as with its accompaniments, it is a meal in itself.

- 4 tablespoons groundnut oil
- 625 g/1¼ lb skinless, boneless chicken breasts, cut into bite-sized pieces
- 1½ teaspoons chilli powder
- ½ teaspoon turmeric
- ½ teaspoon salt
- 600 ml/1 pint coconut milk (see page 7)
- 300 ml/½ pint chicken stock
- 50 g/2 oz creamed coconut, chopped
- 375 g/12 oz cellophane noodles
- sesame oil
- salt

SPICE PASTE:
- 4 large garlic cloves, chopped
- 2 onions, chopped
- 1 large fresh red chilli, deseeded and chopped
- 2.5 cm/1 inch piece of fresh root ginger, chopped
- 1 teaspoon shrimp paste

ACCOMPANIMENTS:
- 3 spring onions, sliced
- 2 tablespoons crisply fried onion flakes (see page 9)
- 3 garlic cloves, sliced and crisply fried
- 2 tablespoons fresh coriander leaves
- 1 lemon, cut into wedges
- whole dried chillies, fried (optional)

1 First make the spice paste. Place the garlic, onions, chilli, ginger and shrimp paste in a food processor or blender and work to a thick paste.
2 Heat the groundnut oil in a large heavy-based saucepan, add the spice paste and fry over gentle heat, stirring constantly, for 5 minutes until softened.
3 Add the chicken pieces to the pan and fry, stirring constantly, for a further 5 minutes to seal. Stir in the chilli powder, turmeric, salt, coconut milk and stock. Bring the curry to the boil, then reduce the heat and simmer very gently, stirring occasionally, for 30 minutes or until the chicken pieces are tender.
4 Stir the creamed coconut into the curry and then simmer over medium heat for 2–3 minutes, stirring the mixture constantly, until the creamed coconut has dissolved and thickened the sauce slightly. Taste and adjust the seasoning if necessary.
5 Drop the noodles into a pan of salted boiling water. Bring the water back to the boil and cook the noodles for 3 minutes. Drain the noodles and stir through a little sesame oil.
6 To serve, divide the noodles among 4 deep soup bowls and ladle some chicken curry over each portion. Serve the accompaniments separately. The fried dried chillies should be nibbled with caution: they are extremely hot!

Serves 4
Preparation time: 15 minutes
Cooking time: 50 minutes

Chicken Korma with Green Beans

This is the perfect curry for those who find chillies too much for them. Korma curry powder is very mild, with little or no chilli, but including coriander, cumin, mustard seeds, fenugreek and bay leaves.

- 2 tablespoons vegetable oil
- 375 g/12 oz skinless, boneless chicken breasts, cut into bite-sized pieces
- 1 onion, sliced
- 2½ tablespoons korma curry powder
- 150 ml/¼ pint chicken stock
- 1 teaspoon tomato purée
- 2 teaspoons caster sugar
- 75 g/3 oz tomatoes, roughly chopped
- 150 ml/¼ pint single cream
- 125 g/4 oz French beans, topped and tailed and cut into 2.5 cm/1 inch lengths
- 25 g/1 oz ground almonds
- salt
- toasted flaked almonds, to garnish

1 Heat the oil in a saucepan, add the chicken and onion, and fry over gentle heat, stirring occasionally, for 6 minutes or until the onion is soft and the chicken is lightly coloured. Stir in the curry powder and cook for a further 2 minutes.
2 Add the stock, tomato purée, sugar, tomatoes, cream and a little salt. Stir to combine the ingredients, bring to the boil, then reduce the heat, cover the pan and simmer gently for 10 minutes, stirring occasionally.
3 Stir the beans into the curry and cook, covered, for a further 15–20 minutes, stirring occasionally, until the chicken is cooked and the beans are tender. Stir the ground almonds into the curry and simmer for 1 minute to thicken the sauce. Taste and adjust the seasoning if necessary. Serve the korma hot, garnished with toasted flaked almonds.

Serves 4
Preparation time: 10–15 minutes
Cooking time: 40 minutes

Chicken Matsaman Curry

Matsaman is a corruption of the word Moslem and reflects the northern Indian influence on this curry from Thailand.

- 3 tablespoons vegetable oil
- 4 chicken drumsticks
- 350 ml/12 fl oz coconut milk (see page 7)
- 1½ tablespoons matsaman curry paste
- 3 new potatoes, scrubbed or peeled
- 1 onion, quartered
- ½ teaspoon lemon juice
- 1½ tablespoons Thai fish sauce (nam pla)
- ½ tablespoon sugar
- 25 g/1 oz roasted peanuts

1 Heat the oil in a large saucepan. Add the chicken drumsticks and brown on all sides. Stir the coconut milk into the pan and bring it to the boil. Add the curry paste. Lower the heat and simmer for 2 hours.
2 Stir in the potatoes, onion, lemon juice, fish sauce, sugar and peanuts, cover the pan and simmer for 20 minutes. Serve immediately.

Serves 4
Preparation time: 15 minutes
Cooking time: about 2½ hours

VARIATION

Beef Matsaman Curry

Replace the chicken with 750 g/1½ lb cubed stewing steak and proceed as in the main recipe.

Thai Green Chicken Curry

- 2 tablespoons groundnut oil
- 2.5 cm/1 inch piece of fresh root ginger, finely chopped
- 2 shallots, chopped
- 4 tablespoons Thai green curry paste (see page 8)
- 625 g/1¼ lb skinless, boneless chicken thighs, cut into 5 cm/2 inch pieces
- 300 ml/½ pint coconut milk (see page 7)
- 4 teaspoons Thai fish sauce (nam pla)
- 1 teaspoon palm sugar or soft brown sugar
- 3 kaffir lime leaves, shredded
- 1 green chilli, deseeded and sliced
- Thai basil leaves, to garnish (optional)

1 Heat the oil in a wok, add the ginger and shallots and fry over a gentle heat, stirring, for about 3 minutes or until softened. Add the green curry paste and fry for a further 2 minutes.

2 Add the chicken to the wok, stir to coat evenly in the spice mixture and fry for 3 minutes to seal the chicken. Stir the coconut milk into the curry, bring it to the boil, then reduce the heat and cook the curry gently, stirring occasionally, for 10 minutes or until the chicken is cooked through and the sauce has thickened.

3 Stir in the fish sauce, sugar, lime leaves and green chilli and cook the curry for a further 5 minutes. Taste and adjust the seasoning, if necessary, and serve the curry immediately, garnished with Thai basil leaves, if liked.

Serves 4
Preparation time: 10 minutes
Cooking time: 25 minutes

Chicken with Cashews

- 4 boneless, skinless chicken breasts, each weighing about 150 g/5 oz
- 2 tablespoons vegetable oil
- 1 bunch spring onions, sliced thinly on the diagonal
- 2 garlic cloves, crushed
- 125 g/4 oz cashews
- pepper

SAUCE:
- 2 teaspoons cornflour
- 6 tablespoons cold chicken stock or water
- 3 tablespoons soy sauce
- 2 tablespoons rice wine or dry sherry
- 2 teaspoons dark soft brown sugar

1 First prepare the sauce. Place the cornflour in a bowl, add 1 tablespoon of the stock or water and work to a paste. Stir in the remaining stock or water, the soy sauce, rice wine or sherry and sugar. Set aside.

2 Cut the chicken breasts into thin strips across the grain. Heat a wok until hot. Add the oil and heat over moderate heat until hot. Add the chicken strips, increase the heat to high and stir-fry for 3–4 minutes or until lightly coloured on all sides, then add the spring onions and garlic. Stir-fry for 1 further minute.

3 Stir the sauce to mix, then pour into the wok. Bring to the boil, stirring constantly. Add the cashews and toss to combine with the chicken and spring onions. Add pepper to taste and serve at once with rice.

Serves 3–4
Preparation time: 10 minutes
Cooking time: 10–15 minutes

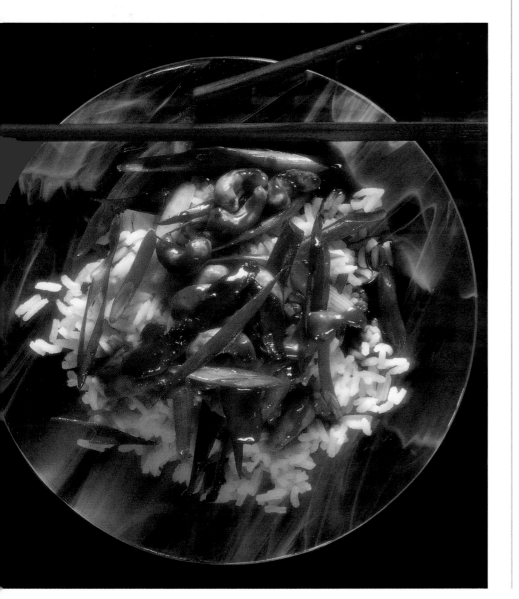

Balti Chicken Vindaloo

- 1½ teaspoons coriander seeds
- 1½ teaspoons cumin seeds
- ¼ teaspoon black onion seeds (kalonji)
- ¼ teaspoon fenugreek seeds
- ¼ teaspoon mustard seeds
- 2.5 cm/1 inch piece of cinnamon stick
- 3 cloves
- ¾ teaspoon peppercorns
- 2 tablespoons desiccated coconut
- 2 tablespoons unsalted peanuts
- 6 tablespoons vinegar
- 2 garlic cloves, crushed
- 1 teaspoon chopped fresh root ginger
- ½ teaspoon turmeric
- 1½ teaspoons chilli powder
- 2 teaspoons salt
- 1.5 kg/3 lb chicken, skinned and cut into pieces
- 3 tablespoons vegetable oil
- 12 curry leaves
- 1 teaspoon cumin seeds
- fried onion rings (see page 8), to garnish

1 Dry roast the coriander, cumin, black onion, fenugreek, mustard, cinnamon, cloves, peppercorns, coconut and peanuts, then grind them in a spice grinder. Transfer to a bowl, then mix in the vinegar, garlic, ginger, turmeric, chilli powder and salt. Spread the mixture over the chicken pieces, cover and leave to marinate overnight.
2 Heat the oil in a Balti pan or wok, then add the curry leaves and cumin seeds. Cook for about 10 seconds, then add the chicken and cook, turning once or twice, for 15 minutes. Cover and continue cooking for a further 15–20 minutes or until the chicken is tender, adding a little water from time to time to keep the chicken moist. Leave over a very low heat for a few minutes before serving, garnished with the fried onion rings.

Serves 4–6
Preparation time: 20 minutes, plus marinating
Cooking time: 30–40 minutes

Chicken with Coconut Milk

- about 3 tablespoons oil
- 4 boneless, skinless chicken breasts, cut into 3 or 4 pieces
- 6 cardamom pods
- 6 cloves
- 5 cm/2 inch piece of cinnamon stick
- 1 large onion, finely sliced
- 2 garlic cloves
- 3.5 cm/1½ inch piece of fresh root ginger, peeled and chopped
- 3 green chillies, seeded
- juice of 1 lemon
- 1 teaspoon turmeric
- 50 g/2 oz creamed coconut
- 150 ml/¼ pint hot water
- salt
- strips of red pepper, to garnish

1 Heat the oil in a heavy-based saucepan, add the chicken and fry quickly all over. Remove with a slotted spoon and set aside.

2 Add a little more oil to the pan if necessary, and fry the cardamom, cloves and cinnamon for 1 minute. Add the onion and sauté gently for about 5 minutes until softened.

3 Place the garlic, ginger, chillies and lemon juice in a food processor or blender and work to a smooth paste. Add to the pan with the turmeric and cook for 5 minutes.

4 Melt the coconut in the hot water and add to the pan with salt to taste. Simmer for 2 minutes, then add the chicken pieces and any juices. Simmer for 15–20 minutes, until tender.

5 Transfer to a warmed serving dish, garnish with red pepper strips and serve immediately.

Serves 4
Preparation time: 10 minutes
Cooking time: 35–40 minutes

Kashmiri Chicken

- 50 g/2 oz ghee or butter
- 3 large onions, finely sliced
- 10 peppercorns
- 10 cardamom pods
- 5 cm/2 inch piece cinnamon stick
- 5 cm/2 inch piece of fresh root ginger, peeled and chopped
- 2 garlic cloves, finely chopped
- 1 teaspoon chilli powder
- 2 teaspoons paprika
- 1.5 kg/3 lb chicken pieces, skinned
- 250 g/8 oz natural yogurt
- salt

TO GARNISH:

- lime wedges
- chopped parsley

1 Melt the ghee or butter in a wok. Add the onions, peppercorns, cardamoms and cinnamon and fry for about 8–10 minutes, stirring occasionally, until the onions are golden. Add the ginger, garlic, chilli powder, paprika and salt to taste and fry for 2 minutes, stirring occasionally.
2 Add the chicken pieces and fry until they are evenly browned. Gradually add the yogurt, stirring constantly. Cover and cook for about 30 minutes, or until the chicken is cooked. Serve hot, garnished with lime wedges and the parsley.

Serves 4–6
Preparation time: 10 minutes
Cooking time: about 40 minutes

Chicken Tikka Masala

- 4 boneless, skinless chicken breasts, cubed
- juice of 1 lemon
- 1½ teaspoons salt
- 2 teaspoons pepper
- 1 onion, quartered
- 2 garlic cloves
- 5 cm/2 inch piece of fresh root ginger, peeled
- 375 g/12 oz natural yogurt
- chopped parsley or fresh coriander, to garnish

MASALA:
- 75 g/3 oz ghee or butter
- 1 onion, thinly sliced
- 1 garlic clove, thinly sliced
- 1½ teaspoons turmeric
- 1½ teaspoons chilli powder
- 1 teaspoon ground cinnamon
- seeds of 20 cardamom pods
- 1 teaspoon ground coriander
- 2 teaspoons aniseed

1 Place the chicken in a bowl and sprinkle with lemon juice, salt and pepper, mix to coat the chicken thoroughly, then cover and set aside.
2 Place the onion, garlic and ginger in a food processor or blender and chop finely. Add the yogurt and strain in the lemon juice from the chicken. Purée until blended, then pour over the chicken. Cover and marinate in the refrigerator for 24 hours.
3 Thread the chicken cubes on to kebab skewers, reserving the marinade. Place under a preheated grill and grill as slowly as possible for about 6–8 minutes until just cooked through. It is important not to overcook the chicken. Remove the chicken from the skewers.
4 Meanwhile, to make the masala, melt the ghee or butter in a wok, add the onion and garlic and fry for 4–5 minutes until soft. Sprinkle on the turmeric, chilli powder and cinnamon, stir well and fry for 1 minute. Add the cardamom, coriander and aniseed and stir-fry for 2 minutes, then add the reserved yogurt marinade. Mix well and bring to the boil. Add the chicken and cook for 5 minutes. Garnish with the chopped parsley and serve at once. Shredded spring onions make a pleasant accompaniment.

Serves 4–6
Preparation time: 45 minutes, plus marinating
Cooking time: about 20 minutes

Chicken Dhansak

- 250 g/8 oz channa dhal
- 250 g/8 oz moong dhal
- 1.2 litres/2 pints water
- 175 g/6 oz ghee
- 2 large onions, peeled and sliced
- 4 garlic cloves, peeled and sliced
- 6 cloves
- 6 cardamom pods
- 1½ teaspoons ground ginger
- 2 teaspoons garam masala
- 2½ teaspoons salt
- 1 chicken, weighing 1.5 kg/3 lb, skinned, boned and cut into 8 pieces
- 500 g/1 lb frozen whole leaf spinach
- 4 large tomatoes, chopped
- fried onion rings (see page 8) to garnish

1 Wash the dhals, place them in a large saucepan and add the water. Bring to the boil and simmer, covered, for 15 minutes.

2 Meanwhile, melt the ghee in a heavy pan, add the onions and garlic and fry gently for about 5 minutes until soft. Add the cloves, cardamom pods, ginger, garam masala and salt and fry for a further 3 minutes, stirring constantly.

3 Add the chicken and fry until browned on all sides, then remove from the pan with a slotted spoon and drain on kitchen paper.

4 Add the spinach and tomatoes to the pan and fry gently for 10 minutes, stirring occasionally.

5 Mash the dhals in the cooking water, then stir into the spinach mixture. Return the chicken to the pan, cover with a tight-fitting lid and simmer for 45 minutes or until the chicken is tender. Serve hot, garnished with fried onion rings.

Serves 4
Preparation time: 15 minutes
Cooking time: 1 hour 10 minutes

Balinese Duck Curry

- 4 tablespoons vegetable oil
- 1.5 kg/3 lb oven-ready duck, cut into 4 portions
- 1 stalk of lemon grass, halved lengthways
- 4 kaffir lime leaves, bruised
- 1 teaspoon salt
- 300 ml/½ pint water
- 2 teaspoons soft brown sugar
- 2 green chillies, sliced, to garnish

SPICE PASTE:
- 8 shallots, chopped
- 4 garlic cloves, chopped
- 6 large green chillies, deseeded and chopped, extra to garnish
- 5 cm/2 inch piece of fresh root ginger, chopped
- 2.5 cm/1 inch piece of fresh galangal, chopped
- 2 teaspoons turmeric
- ¼ teaspoon pepper
- 6 candlenuts or macadamia nuts (optional)

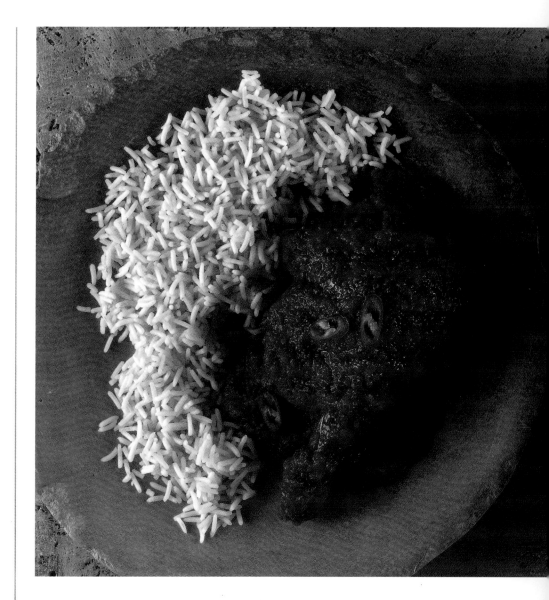

1 First make the spice paste. Put the shallots, garlic, green chillies, ginger, galangal, tumeric, pepper and candlenuts or macadamia nuts, if using, into a food processor or blender and work to a thick paste. Heat the vegetable oil in a wide sauté pan, add the paste and fry over gentle heat, stirring constantly, for about 3 minutes or until softened and fragrant.
2 Add the duck portions, lemon grass, lime leaves and salt to the pan. Stir to coat the duck evenly in the spice mixture and fry for a further 4 minutes to seal the meat. Add the water, stir well and bring to the boil. Reduce the heat, cover the pan and cook gently, stirring from time to time, for 45 minutes, until the duck is tender.
3 Remove the lid from the pan, stir in the sugar and increase the heat to moderate. Cook, stirring frequently, for a further 30 minutes, until the duck is cooked and the sauce is thick.
4 Skim off any surplus fat from the surface of the curry. Taste and adjust the seasoning if necessary. Serve hot, garnished with sliced chillies.

Serves 4
Preparation time: 25 minutes
Cooking time: 1½ hours

Meat Dishes

Pork in Coconut Milk

A Nonya dish from Malaysia, blending two cuisines – the Chinese love of pork and the Malaysian use of coconut milk.

2 onions, peeled and quartered

8 dried red chillies

6 macadamia nuts

½ teaspoon terasi (dried shrimp paste)

2 tablespoons vegetable oil

750 g/1½ lb lean pork, cut into 2.5 cm/1 inch cubes

250 ml/8 fl oz water

1 teaspoon salt

250 ml/8 fl oz thick coconut milk (see page 7)

1 tablespoon sugar

2 tablespoons lime or lemon juice

TO GARNISH:

dried red chillies

slices of fresh coconut

sprigs of fresh coriander

1 Put the onions, chillies, macadamia nuts, terasi and 1 tablespoon water into a food processor or blender and grind to a paste.

2 Heat the oil in a large saucepan and gently fry the paste, stirring, for 3–4 minutes. Add the pork and cook, stirring, until it changes colour and is well coated with the paste.

3 Pour in the water and add the salt. Cover and simmer gently for about 30 minutes until the pork is just tender.

4 Add the coconut milk and simmer uncovered for 10–15 minutes, stirring from time to time. Stir in the sugar and lime juice.

5 To serve, spoon the curry into individual bowls and garnish with dried chilli strips, fresh coconut and coriander sprigs.

Serves 4–6
Preparation time: 30 minutes
Cooking time: about 45 minutes

Raan

This is a dish for special occasions and, although it takes time to prepare with the lengthy marinating and slow roasting, it is quite simple to make. The two applications of spice paste give it a subtle depth of flavour.

- 2.5 kg/5 lb leg of lamb, skin and fat removed
- 50 g/2 oz piece of fresh root ginger, peeled and chopped
- 6 garlic cloves
- rind of 1 lemon
- juice of 2 lemons
- 2 teaspoons cumin seeds
- 6 cardamom pods, peeled
- 1 teaspoon ground cloves
- 1 teaspoon turmeric
- 1½ teaspoons chilli powder
- 1 tablespoon salt
- 300 g/10 oz natural yogurt
- 150 g/5 oz whole, unpeeled almonds
- 4 tablespoons brown sugar
- 1 teaspoon saffron threads, soaked in 3 tablespoons boiling water

TO GARNISH:
- mint leaves
- lime slices

1 Prick the lamb all over with a fork and make about 12 deep cuts in the flesh. Place the ginger, garlic, lemon rind and juice, cumin seeds, cardamom pods, cloves, turmeric, chilli powder and salt in a food processor or blender and work to a paste. Spread the paste over the lamb and leave to stand, covered, for 1 hour in a flameproof casserole.

2 Blend 4 tablespoons of the yogurt with the almonds and 2 tablespoons of sugar. Stir in the remaining yogurt and pour over the lamb. Cover tightly and chill for 48 hours in the refrigerator.
3 Let the meat return to room temperature. Sprinkle with the rest of the sugar and cook, uncovered, in a preheated oven, 220°C (425°F), Gas Mark 7, for 30 minutes. Cover the casserole, lower the heat to 160°C (325°F), Gas Mark 3 and cook for 3 hours, basting occasionally. Sprinkle with the saffron water and cook for a further 30 minutes or until very tender.

4 Remove the meat from the casserole, wrap it in foil and keep warm. Skim off the fat from the casserole and boil the sauce until thick. Place the meat on a dish and pour over the sauce. Carve in thick slices to serve, and garnish with mint and lime slices.

Serves 6
Preparation time: 20 minutes, plus standing and marinating
Cooking time: about 4 hours
Oven temperature: 220°C (425°F), Gas Mark 7; then 160°C (325°F), Gas Mark 3

Lamb with Yogurt

- 4 tablespoons oil
- 3 onions, finely chopped
- 6 cardamom pods
- 5 cm/2 inch piece of cinnamon stick
- 1½ tablespoons ground coriander
- 2 teaspoons ground cumin
- ½ teaspoon turmeric
- ½ teaspoon ground cloves
- 1–2 teaspoons chilli powder
- ½ teaspoon grated nutmeg

- 1 tablespoon paprika
- 300 g/10 oz natural yogurt
- 750 g/1½ lb boned leg of lamb, cubed
- 1 large tomato, skinned and chopped
- salt
- sprigs of fennel, to garnish

1 Heat the oil in a large saucepan, add the onions, cardamom and cinnamon and fry for about 5 minutes.
2 Stir in the coriander, cumin, turmeric, cloves, chilli powder and nutmeg and fry until dry, then add

2 tablespoons water and cook, stirring, for 5 minutes, adding a little more water if necessary.
3 Add the paprika and slowly stir in the yogurt. Add the lamb, tomato and salt to taste and mix well. Bring to simmering point, cover and cook for 1 hour or until tender. Garnish with the fennel sprigs to serve.

Serves 4
Preparation time: 15 minutes
Cooking time: 1¼ hours

Roghan Ghosht

One of the best known of all curries from northern India.

- 4 tablespoons oil
- 2 onions, finely chopped
- 750 g/1½ lb boned leg of lamb, cubed
- 300 g/10 oz natural yogurt
- 2 garlic cloves
- 2.5 cm/1 inch piece of fresh root ginger, peeled and roughly chopped
- 2 green chillies, deseeded
- 1 tablespoon coriander seeds
- 1 teaspoon cumin seeds
- 1 teaspoon chopped mint leaves
- 1 teaspoon chopped fresh coriander
- 6 cardamom pods
- 6 cloves
- 2.5 cm/1 inch piece of cinnamon stick
- salt and pepper
- 125 g/4 oz flaked almonds

TO GARNISH:
- fried onion rings (see page 8)
- lemon slices

1 Heat 2 tablespoons of the oil in a large saucepan, add half of the onions and fry until golden.

2 Add the lamb and 175 g/6 oz of the yogurt, stir well, cover and simmer for 20 minutes.

3 Meanwhile, place the garlic, ginger, chillies, coriander seeds, cumin, mint, fresh coriander and 2–3 tablespoons of the yogurt in a food processor or blender and work to a paste.

4 Heat the remaining oil in a large saucepan, add the cardamom, cloves and cinnamon and fry for 1 minute, stirring. Add the remaining onion and the prepared spice paste and fry for 5 minutes, stirring constantly.

5 Add the lamb and yogurt mixture, season to taste, stir well and bring to simmering point. Cover and cook for 30 minutes.

6 Add the almonds and cook for a further 15 minutes, until the meat is tender. Garnish with fried onion rings and lemon slices and and serve immediately.

Serves 4
Preparation time: 20 minutes
Cooking time: about 1¼ hours

Kheema Dopiazah

Dopiazah describes a dish which contains double the normal quantity of onions. *Doh* means two or twice, and *piazah* means onions. The main feature of the *dopiazah* is that some of the onions are cooked with the meat, while the rest are added later to provide a contrast in texture.

- 500 g/1 lb onions
- 4 tablespoons oil
- 2.5 cm/1 inch piece of fresh root ginger, peeled and chopped
- 1 garlic clove, finely chopped
- 2 green chillies, finely chopped
- 1 teaspoon turmeric
- 1 teaspoon ground coriander seeds
- 1 teaspoon ground cumin seeds
- 750 g/1½ lb minced lamb
- 150 g/5 oz natural yogurt
- 1 x 225 g/7½ oz can tomatoes
- salt
- chopped fresh parsley, to garnish

1 Finely chop 375 g/12 oz of the onions and thinly slice the remainder.
2 Heat 2 tablespoons of the oil in a large heavy-based saucepan, add the chopped onion and fry until golden. Add the ginger, garlic, chillies, turmeric, coriander and cumin and fry for 2 minutes. Add the lamb and cook, stirring, until well browned.
3 Stir in the yogurt, a spoonful at a time, until it is absorbed, then add the tomatoes with their juices, and salt to taste. Bring to the boil, stir well, then cover the pan and simmer for 20 minutes or until the meat is cooked.

4 Meanwhile, heat the remaining oil in a frying pan and fry the sliced onions until brown and crisp. To serve, transfer the meat mixture to a warmed serving dish and sprinkle with the fried onion and chopped parsley.

Serves 4
Preparation time: 20 minutes
Cooking time: about 50 minutes

Balti Kheema

- 2 tablespoons vegetable oil
- 500 g/1 lb green peppers, cored, deseeded and sliced
- 500 g/1 lb onions, sliced
- 2 teaspoons salt
- 2 teaspoons pepper
- ½ teaspoon ground cumin
- 2 teaspoons garam masala
- pinch of ground cinnamon
- 1½ teaspoons chilli powder
- 750 g/1½ lb minced lamb
- red onion rings, to garnish

1 Heat the oil in a Balti pan or heavy-based frying pan, add the peppers and stir-fry for about 1 minute. Remove the peppers with a slotted spoon and keep warm.
2 Add the onions to the oil and fry until they are golden brown. Add the salt, pepper, cumin, garam masala, cinnamon and chilli powder and stir-fry for 2 minutes.
3 Add the minced lamb and cook gently for about 20 minutes, stirring frequently to make sure that it does not stick to the bottom of the pan.
4 Return the green peppers to the pan and heat through over a low heat for a further 10 minutes. Garnish with onion rings and serve with poppadums.

Serves 4–6
Preparation time: 15 minutes
Cooking time: 35 minutes

Lamb Curry with Coconut

If fresh coconut is not available, blend the other spices and lemon juice as in step 1 and add 50 g/2 oz creamed coconut to the onions with the blended spices.

- 4 tablespoons oil
- 2 onions, chopped
- 4 curry leaves
- 750 g/1½ lb boned leg of lamb, cubed
- 1 x 225 g/ 7½ oz can tomatoes
- salt

SPICE PASTE:
- grated flesh of ½ fresh coconut
- 4 dried red chillies
- 1 teaspoon cumin seeds
- 1 tablespoon coriander seeds
- 1 tablespoon poppy seeds
- 1 teaspoon peppercorns
- 2.5 cm/1 inch piece of fresh root ginger, peeled and chopped
- 2 garlic cloves
- 1 teaspoon turmeric
- 2 tablespoons lemon juice

TO GARNISH:
- grated coconut
- 2 tablespoons finely chopped fresh coriander

1 First make the spice paste. Put the coconut, chillies, cumin, coriander and poppy seeds in a frying pan and dry-fry for about 1 minute. Place in a food processor or blender with the peppercorns, ginger, garlic, turmeric and lemon juice and blend to a paste.
2 Heat the oil in a large saucepan, add the onions and fry for about 5 minutes until softened, then add the curry leaves and the prepared spice paste and fry for 5 minutes.
3 Add the lamb and cook, stirring, for 5 minutes, then add the tomatoes with their juices and season with salt to taste. Bring to simmering point, cover and cook for about 1 hour, until tender.
4 To serve, sprinkle with grated coconut and chopped fresh coriander.

Serves 4
Preparation time: 20 minutes
Cooking time: about 1 hour 10 minutes

Stir-fried Lamb with Okra and Tomatoes

- 250 g/8 oz small okra, trimmed
- 3 tablespoons vegetable oil
- 1 onion, thinly sliced
- 1–2 garlic cloves, crushed
- 2 teaspoons ground coriander
- 2 teaspoons turmeric
- 1 teaspoon hot chilli powder, or to taste
- 500 g/1 lb lamb fillet, cut into thin strips across the grain
- 250 g/8 oz ripe tomatoes, skinned and chopped roughly
- finely grated rind and juice of ½ lemon
- ½ teaspoon caster sugar
- salt

1 Blanch the okra in boiling salted water for 5 minutes, then drain, rinse under cold running water and drain again. Set aside.

2 Heat a wok until hot. Add the oil and heat over moderate heat until hot. Add the onion, garlic, coriander, turmeric and chilli powder and stir-fry for 2–3 minutes or until the onion is softened, taking care not to let any of the ingredients brown.

3 Add the lamb strips, increase the heat to high and stir-fry for 3–4 minutes or until the lamb is browned on all sides.

4 Add the tomatoes and stir-fry until the juices run, then add the lemon rind and juice, sugar and salt to taste. Stir-fry to mix, then add the okra and toss for 3–4 minutes or until heated through. Serve hot with boiled rice.

Serves 4
Preparation time: 10 minutes
Cooking time: about 15 minutes

Thai Red Beef Curry

It is easy to produce an 'authentic' curry quickly, using either your own homemade Thai red curry paste, or one of the excellent ready-made versions now stocked by Asian shops and many supermarkets.

- 3 tablespoons groundnut oil
- 3 tablespoons Thai red curry paste (see page 7)
- ½ teaspoon ground coriander
- ½ teaspoon ground cumin
- 4 Kaffir lime leaves, shredded

- 500 g/1 lb fillet of beef, cut into thin strips
- 400 ml/14 fl oz coconut milk (see page 7)
- 2 tablespoons crunchy peanut butter
- 2 teaspoons Thai fish sauce (nam pla)
- 1 tablespoon soft brown sugar
- sprigs of coriander, to garnish (optional)

1 Heat the oil in a heavy-based saucepan and add the red curry paste, ground coriander and cumin and the lime leaves. Cook over gentle heat, stirring frequently, for 3 minutes.
2 Add the beef strips to the pan, stir to coat them evenly in the curry paste and cook gently, stirring frequently for 5 minutes.
3 Add half of the coconut milk to the pan, stir to combine and simmer gently for 4 minutes until most of the coconut milk has been absorbed.
4 Stir in the rest of the coconut milk with the peanut butter, fish sauce and sugar. Simmer gently for 5 minutes until the sauce is thick and the beef is tender. Garnish with coriander sprigs, if using, and serve immediately with steamed rice.

Serves 4
Preparation time: 5–10 minutes
Cooking time: about 20 minutes

Malaysian Beef and Potato Curry

- 2 tablespoons groundnut oil
- 5 shallots, chopped
- 2 garlic cloves, crushed
- 5 cm/2 inch piece of fresh root ginger, grated
- 2 tablespoons hot curry powder
- 1 teaspoon ground cinnamon
- 1 teaspoon ground cumin
- 1 teaspoon ground coriander
- ¼ teaspoon ground cardamom
- 4 curry leaves
- 1 star anise
- 4 cloves
- 375 g/12 oz sirloin steak, cut into 1 cm/½ inch strips
- 300 g/10 oz potatoes, peeled and cut into medium chunks
- 2 large red chillies, deseeded and finely chopped
- ½ teaspoon salt
- 300 ml/½ pint coconut milk (see page 7)
- juice of 1 lime
- 1 teaspoon soft brown sugar
- sliced red chillies, to garnish

1 Heat the oil in a saucepan, add the shallots, garlic and ginger, and fry over a gentle heat, stirring frequently, for 5 minutes or until softened.

2 Add the curry powder, cinnamon, cumin, coriander, cardamom, curry leaves, star anise and cloves, and fry for 1 minute.

3 Add the beef and stir well to coat it in the spice mixture. Add the potatoes, chillies, salt and coconut milk. Stir to combine, bring to the boil, then reduce the heat, cover the pan and simmer gently, stirring occasionally, for 40 minutes until the beef is tender and the potatoes are cooked.

4 Stir in the lime juice and sugar and cook uncovered for 2 minutes. Taste and adjust the seasoning, if necessary, and serve hot, garnished with sliced red chillies.

Serves 4

Preparation time: 20 minutes
Cooking time: 50 minutes

Simple Beef Curry with Spinach

If you would like to make this curry hotter, add some of the seeds from the green chillies to it.

- 2 tablespoons ghee or vegetable oil
- 1 large onion, thinly sliced
- 2 garlic cloves, crushed
- 2 green chillies, deseeded and sliced
- 2 cloves, bruised
- 1 teaspoon garam masala
- 1 teaspoon ground coriander
- 1 teaspoon turmeric
- ½ teaspoon chilli powder
- 1½ teaspoons ground cumin
- 625 g/1¼ lb fillet of beef, cut into bite-sized pieces
- 1 teaspoon salt
- 175 g/6 oz tomatoes, cut into large dice
- 150 ml/¼ pint coconut milk (see page 7)
- 250 g/8 oz ready-washed young leaf spinach
- 1 teaspoon lemon juice

1 Heat the ghee or oil in a saucepan, add the onion and garlic and fry over a gentle heat, stirring frequently, for about 5 minutes or until softened but not coloured. Stir in the chillies and fry for 2 minutes.

2 Add the cloves, garam masala, coriander, turmeric, chilli powder and cumin. Stir well to mix and fry, stirring constantly, for 2 minutes.

3 Stir in the beef and salt and cook, stirring, for 3 minutes to seal the meat, then add the diced tomatoes, coconut milk and spinach and stir to mix.

Cover the pan and simmer gently, stirring very occasionally, for 20 minutes.

4 Stir in the lemon juice and cook the curry, uncovered, for a further 8–10 minutes, stirring occasionally, until the sauce has thickened. Taste and adjust the seasoning if necessary and serve immediately. Saffron rice would be a good accompaniment to this curry.

Serves 4
Preparation time: about 20 minutes
Cooking time: 35–40 minutes

Chilli Fry

This is a fairly dry curry, so take care not to let it stick to the pan.

- 4 tablespoons oil
- 1 large onion, finely chopped
- ½ teaspoon ground coriander seeds
- ½ teaspoon turmeric
- 2.5 cm/1 inch piece of fresh root ginger, finely chopped
- 1 chilli, chopped
- 500 g/1 lb frying steak, cut into 2.5 x 1 cm/ 1 x ½ inch strips
- 1 green or red pepper, cored, deseeded and roughly chopped
- 2 tomatoes, quartered
- juice of 1 lemon
- salt

1 Heat the oil in a wok or frying pan, add the onion and fry for about 5 minutes until softened. Add the coriander, turmeric, ginger and chilli and fry over low heat for 5 minutes; if the mixture becomes dry, add 1 tablespoon water.
2 Add the steak, increase the heat and cook, stirring, until browned all over. Add the chopped pepper, cover and simmer gently for 5–10 minutes, until the meat is tender. Add the tomatoes, lemon juice and salt to taste and cook, uncovered, for 2–3 minutes.

Serves 4
Preparation time: 10–15 minutes
Cooking time: 25–30 minutes

Nargis Kebab

This is an Indian version of the Scotch egg – and may be served with or without the sauce.

- 250 g/8 oz minced beef
- 2 garlic cloves, crushed
- 2.5 cm/1 inch piece of fresh root ginger, peeled and grated
- ½ teaspoon ground coriander seeds
- ½ teaspoon ground cumin seeds
- ½–1 teaspoon chilli powder
- ¼ teaspoon ground cloves
- 1 tablespoon cornflour
- salt
- 1 egg yolk
- 4 small hard-boiled eggs
- oil, for shallow frying

SAUCE:

- 4 tablespoons oil
- 5 cm/2 inch piece of cinnamon stick
- 6 cloves
- 6 cardamom pods
- 1 onion, finely chopped
- 2 garlic cloves, crushed
- 2.5 cm/1 inch piece of fresh root ginger, peeled and grated
- 2 teaspoons ground coriander seeds
- 1 teaspoon ground cumin seeds
- ½–1 teaspoon chilli powder
- 4 tablespoons natural yogurt
- 1 x 400 g/13 oz can tomatoes
- 2 tablespoons chopped fresh coriander

1 To make the kebabs, mix together the beef, garlic, ginger, coriander seeds, cumin, chilli powder, cloves and cornflour and add salt to taste. Bind with the egg yolk and divide the mixture into 4 equal parts.

2 With well-floured hands, flatten each portion into a round, place a hard-boiled egg in the centre and work the meat around to cover. Roll each one into a ball.

3 Heat the oil in a pan and shallow fry the kebabs until they are brown all over. Lift out with a slotted spoon and drain on kitchen paper. Set aside while making the sauce.

4 To make the sauce, heat the oil in a saucepan, add the cinnamon, cloves and cardamom and fry for a few seconds. Add the onion, garlic and ginger and fry until golden brown. Add the coriander seeds, cumin and chilli powder and fry for 1 minute. Add the yogurt, a spoonful at a time, stirring until it is absorbed before adding the next spoonful.

5 Break up the tomatoes with a fork, add them to the pan with their juices and simmer for 1 minute. Add the kebabs to the sauce, season with salt to taste and cook, uncovered, for 25 minutes until the sauce is thick. Stir in the chopped coriander to serve.

Serves 4

Preparation time: 15–20 minutes
Cooking time: about 45 minutes

Thai Fried Red Curry with Pork and Beans

- 175 g/6 oz French or runner beans, cut into 2.5 cm/1 inch lengths
- 2 tablespoons vegetable oil
- 300 g/10 oz pork fillet, thinly sliced
- 2 tablespoons Thai red curry paste (see page 7)
- 1 tablespoon Thai fish sauce (nam pla)
- 1 tablespoon demerara sugar

1 Place the beans in a medium saucepan. Add water to cover and bring to the boil. Cook for 5 minutes, then drain thoroughly in a colander. Set aside.

2 Heat the oil in a wok, add the pork and stir-fry for 6–8 minutes or until the pork is cooked. Using a slotted spoon, transfer the pork to a plate and set aside.

3 Add the curry paste to the oil remaining in the pan. Stir-fry for 3 minutes, then return the pork to the pan together with the fish sauce, sugar and cooked beans. Stir-fry for 10 minutes. Serve hot with boiled rice.

Serves 4
Preparation time: 10 minutes
Cooking time: 25–30 minutes

Brinjal Cutlets

In India, croquettes and patties of various sorts are known as cutlets.

- 2 large aubergines
- 3 tablespoons oil
- 1 onion, finely chopped
- 1 garlic clove, finely chopped
- 2 green chillies, deseeded and finely chopped
- 1 teaspoon turmeric
- 500 g/1 lb minced beef
- 1 egg, lightly beaten
- 2–3 tablespoons fresh breadcrumbs
- salt
- chopped fresh coriander, to garnish

1 Place the aubergines in a pan of boiling water and cook for 15 minutes or until they are almost tender. Drain them thoroughly in a colander and leave to cool.

2 Heat the oil in a saucepan, add the onion and fry until golden. Add the garlic, chillies and turmeric and fry for 2 minutes. Add the minced beef and cook, stirring, until brown all over. Add salt to taste and cook gently for 20 minutes until the meat is tender.

3 Cut the aubergines in half lengthways. Carefully scoop out the pulp, add it to the meat mixture and mix well. Taste and adjust the seasoning.

4 Using a spoon, carefully fill the aubergine shells with the mixture, brush with the egg and cover with breadcrumbs. Place the aubergines on a grill rack and cook under a preheated moderate grill for 4–5 minutes, until golden. Garnish with the chopped fresh coriander and serve at once with chilli sauce, if you like.

Serves 4
Preparation time: 10 minutes, plus cooling
Cooking time: 45 minutes

Burmese Pork Curry

- 2 tablespoons ghee
- 2 small onions, each cut into 8 wedges
- 4 garlic cloves, finely chopped
- 5 cm/2 inch piece of fresh root ginger, finely chopped

- 500 g/1 lb pork tenderloin, cut into 2.5 cm/1 inch cubes
- 1 teaspoon turmeric
- ½ teaspoon soft brown sugar
- 1 tablespoon mild curry paste
- 4 dried chillies, soaked in cold water for 10 minutes, then drained and finely chopped
- 2 stalks of lemon grass, quartered lengthways

- 1 teaspoon shrimp paste
- 150 ml/¼ pint vegetable stock
- 2 teaspoons soy sauce
- 2 fresh red chillies, thinly sliced, to garnish

1 Heat the ghee in a heavy-based saucepan, add the onion, garlic, ginger and pork and fry over a brisk heat, stirring constantly, for 4 minutes until lightly golden.

2 Lower the heat, stir in the turmeric, sugar, curry paste, dried chillies, lemon grass and shrimp paste and fry for 2 minutes.

3 Add the stock and soy sauce to the pan, stir to mix well, then bring the curry to the boil. Cover the pan, reduce the heat and cook the curry gently for 30 minutes, stirring occasionally, until the pork is tender. Discard the stalks of lemon grass. Taste, and adjust the seasoning if necessary. Serve the curry hot on a bed of flat rice noodles and garnish with the sliced red chillies.

Serves 4
Preparation time: 10 minutes
Cooking time: 45 minutes

Pork with Tamarind

- 50 g/2 oz dried tamarind
- 75 g/3 oz ghee or butter
- 2 large onions, sliced
- 8 garlic cloves, sliced
- 750 g/1½ lb lean pork, cubed
- ½ teaspoon paprika
- ½ teaspoon turmeric
- 1 teaspoon fenugreek seeds
- 25 g/1 oz fresh root ginger, peeled and chopped
- 2 fresh green chillies
- 1 teaspoon salt
- 1½ teaspoons garam masala
- 2 bay leaves
- 6 cardamom pods
- 3 cloves
- sprigs of coriander, to garnish

1 Put the tamarind into a bowl and pour over 300 ml/½ pint boiling water. Leave to soak for 30 minutes.
2 Melt the ghee or butter in a wok or heavy-based frying pan, add the onions and garlic and fry for 5 minutes until soft, then add the pork and stir-fry to seal the meat on all sides.
3 Add the paprika, turmeric, fenugreek, ginger, chillies and salt. Pour in 150 ml/¼ pint water, cover and cook for 20–30 minutes.

4 Mash the tamarind in the soaking water, then strain through a wire sieve set over a bowl, pressing the tamarind to extract as much pulp as possible.
5 Uncover the wok, bring to the boil and boil until nearly all the liquid has evaporated. Add the garam masala, bay leaves, cardamom pods, cloves and the tamarind pulp and cook over very low heat for about 30 minutes or until the pork is tender. Serve hot, garnished with the coriander sprigs.

Serves 4–6
Preparation time: 20 minutes, plus soaking
Cooking time: about 1¼ hours

Vegetable Dishes

Aubergines with Tomatoes

750 g/1½ lb aubergines, cut into 4 cm/1½ inch chunks

juice of 1 lemon

175 g/6 oz ghee or butter

2 onions, thinly sliced

4 garlic cloves, thinly sliced

7.5 cm/3 inch piece of fresh root ginger, peeled and thinly sliced

2 teaspoons black onion seeds (kalonji)

7.5 cm/3 inch piece cinnamon stick

2 teaspoons coriander seeds

2 teaspoons cumin seeds

2 teaspoons pepper

2 teaspoons salt

2 teaspoons garam masala

1½ teaspoons ground turmeric

1 teaspoon chilli powder

1 x 400 g/13 oz can chopped tomatoes

125 g/4 oz tomato purée

600 ml/1 pint boiling water

dried red chillies, to garnish

1 Place the aubergines in a bowl and stir in the lemon juice.

2 Melt the ghee or butter in a large wok, add the onions, garlic and ginger and fry gently for 4–5 minutes until soft. Add the black onion seeds, cinnamon, coriander and cumin seeds and stir well. Fry for a further 2 minutes, then stir in the pepper, salt, garam masala, turmeric and chilli powder.

3 Add the tomatoes with their juices and the tomato purée, stir well and bring to the boil. Pour in the boiling water and stir in the aubergine pieces with the lemon juice. Bring to the boil, lower the heat and simmer gently for 15–20 minutes until soft. Garnish with the dried red chillies and serve hot.

Serves 4–6
Preparation time: 15 minutes
Cooking time: 25–30 minutes

Spinach Paneer

Paneer is an Indian curd cheese available from all good Indian grocers.

- 250 g/8 oz paneer, cut into 2.5 cm/1 inch cubes
- 375 g/12 oz young leaf spinach, washed and dried
- 2 tablespoons ghee
- 1 large onion, chopped
- 2 garlic cloves, crushed
- 1 large green chilli, deseeded and sliced
- 1 tablespoon grated fresh root ginger
- 1 teaspoon turmeric
- 1 teaspoon ground coriander
- 1 teaspoon chilli powder
- ½ teaspoon ground cumin
- ½ teaspoon salt

1 Cut the paneer into 2.5 cm/1 inch cubes and set it aside. Steam the spinach for 3–4 minutes until it has wilted, leave it to cool and then place it in a food processor and blend briefly to a purée. Set aside.

2 Heat the ghee in a heavy-based saucepan, add the paneer cubes and fry, turning occasionally, for 10 minutes or until they are golden all over. Remove them from the pan with a slotted spoon and set aside.

3 Add the onion, garlic, chilli and ginger to the hot ghee and fry gently over low heat, stirring constantly, for 5 minutes until softened. Stir in the turmeric, ground coriander, chilli powder and cumin, and fry for 1 further minute.

4 Add the puréed spinach and the salt, stir well to combine, cover the pan and simmer gently for 5 minutes.

5 Stir in the fried paneer and cook, covered, for a further 5 minutes. Taste and adjust the seasoning if necessary, and serve immediately.

Serves 4
Preparation time: 15 minutes
Cooking time: 30 minutes

Kidney Bean Curry

- 125 ml/4 fl oz vegetable oil
- 2 teaspoons cumin seeds
- 1 large onion, chopped
- 1 x 400 g/13 oz can chopped tomatoes
- 1 tablespoon ground coriander
- 1 teaspoon chilli powder
- 1 teaspoon sugar
- 1 teaspoon salt
- 2 x 475 g/15 oz cans red kidney beans, drained

1 Heat the oil in a wok or frying pan, add the cumin seeds and chopped onion and fry until the onion is lightly browned. Stir in the tomatoes and fry for a few seconds, then add the ground coriander, chilli powder, sugar and salt and stir well. Lower the heat and cook for about 5–7 minutes. Add the drained kidney beans, stir carefully but thoroughly and cook for 10–15 minutes. Serve immediately with rice.

Serves 4–6
Preparation time: 15 minutes
Cooking time: 30–35 minutes

Vegetables in Malaysian Coconut Sauce

This is a light and simple dish – and you can vary the vegetables according to what is available in the shops or in your garden.

- 125 g/4 oz broccoli florets
- 125 g/4 oz French beans, cut into 2.5 cm/ 1 inch lengths
- 1 red pepper, cored, deseeded and sliced
- 125 g/4 oz courgettes, thinly sliced

MALAYSIAN COCONUT SAUCE:
- 25 g/1 oz dried tamarind
- 150 ml/¼ pint boiling water
- 1 x 425 g/14 oz can thick coconut milk
- 2 teaspoons Thai green curry paste (see page 8)
- 1 teaspoon grated ginger
- 1 onion, diced
- ½ teaspoon turmeric
- salt

1 First make the Malaysian coconut sauce. Put the tamarind into a bowl. Pour over the boiling water and leave to soak for 30 minutes.
2 Mash the tamarind in the soaking water, then strain through a wire sieve set over a bowl, pressing the tamarind to extract as much pulp as possible.
3 Skim 2 tablespoons of the cream from the coconut milk and place it in a wok or heavy-based saucepan. Add the curry paste, ginger, onion and turmeric and cook over gentle heat, stirring for 2–3 minutes. Stir in the remaining coconut milk and the tamarind water. Bring to the boil, then lower the heat and season with salt.
4 Add the broccoli and cook for 5 minutes, then add the French beans and red pepper and cook, stirring, for a further 5 minutes. Finally, stir in the courgettes and cook for 1–2 minutes. Prawn crackers make a nice accompaniment.

Serves 4
Preparation time: 15 minutes, plus standing
Cooking time: about 20 minutes

Masoor Dhal

- 4 tablespoons oil
- 3 cloves
- 2 teaspoons ground coriander
- 1 teaspoon turmeric
- 6 cardamom pods
- 2.5 cm/1 inch piece of cinnamon stick
- 1 onion, chopped
- 2.5 cm/1 inch piece of fresh root ginger, chopped
- 1 green chilli, finely chopped
- 1 garlic clove, chopped
- ½ teaspoon garam masala
- 250 g/8 oz masoor dhal (red split lentils)
- salt
- juice of 1 lemon
- sprigs of marjoram, to garnish

1 Heat the oil in a pan, add the cloves, ground coriander, turmeric, cardamom pods and cinnamon and fry until they start to swell. Add the onion and fry for about 5 minutes until translucent.
2 Add the ginger, chilli, garlic and garam masala and cook for 5 minutes.
3 Add the lentils, stir thoroughly and fry for 1 minute. Season to taste with salt and add enough water to come about 3 cm/1¼ inches above the level of the lentils. Bring to the boil, cover the pan and simmer for about 20 minutes, until the dhal is really thick and the lentils are tender.
4 Sprinkle with the lemon juice and stir to mix. Garnish with marjoram and serve immediately.

Serves 4

Preparation time: 15 minutes
Cooking time: about 35 minutes

Sweet Potato and Spinach Curry

- 500 g/1 lb sweet potato, peeled and cut into large chunks
- 3 tablespoons groundnut oil
- 1 red onion, chopped
- 2 garlic cloves, crushed
- 1 teaspoon shrimp paste
- 1 teaspoon turmeric
- 1 large fresh red chilli, deseeded and chopped
- 400 ml/14 fl oz coconut milk (see page 7)
- 250 g/8 oz ready-washed young leaf spinach
- salt

1 Cook the sweet potato chunks in a pan of salted boiling water for 8–10 minutes or until tender. Drain and set on one side.

2 Heat the oil in a saucepan, add the onion, garlic, shrimp paste and turmeric and fry over a gentle heat, stirring frequently, for 3 minutes. Stir in the chopped red chilli and fry for a further 2 minutes.

3 Add the coconut milk, stir to mix, and simmer for 3–4 minutes until the coconut milk has thickened slightly. Stir in the sweet potatoes, add salt to taste, and cook for 4 minutes.

4 Stir in the spinach, cover the pan and simmer gently for 2–3 minutes or until the spinach has wilted and the curry has heated through. Taste and adjust the seasoning if necessary and serve at once with naan or chapati.

Serves 4
Preparation time: about 10 minutes
Cooking time: about 25 minutes

New Potato Curry

- 5 cm/2 inch piece of fresh root ginger, peeled and grated
- 2 garlic cloves, crushed
- 50 g/2 oz ghee or butter
- 2 large onions, finely chopped
- 2 bay leaves
- 1 cinnamon stick, broken into short lengths
- 2 teaspoons fennel seeds
- 3 green cardamom pods
- 1 teaspoon turmeric
- 1 kg/2 lb small new potatoes, scrubbed
- 600 ml/1 pint water
- 300 ml/½ pint natural yogurt
- salt and pepper

TO GARNISH:
- chilli powder (optional)
- sprigs of coriander

1 Mix together the grated ginger and crushed garlic in a small bowl.
2 Place the ghee or butter in a large saucepan or wok and heat. Add the chopped onions, the ginger mixture, bay leaves, broken cinnamon stick, fennel seeds, cardamoms and turmeric to the melted fat. Fry the mixture gently, stirring constantly, until the onion is soft but not browned.
3 Add the potatoes to the pan, pour in the water and season to taste. Bring to the boil then cover the pan.
4 Simmer the curry steadily for 10 minutes, then uncover the pan and cook fairly rapidly for a further 10 minutes or until most of the water has evaporated.
5 Pour the natural yogurt over the potatoes and heat through fairly gently, to avoid curdling the sauce.

6 Transfer the curry to a serving dish and sprinkle with chilli powder to taste, if using, and coriander sprigs before serving.

Serves 4
Preparation time: 10 minutes
Cooking time: 30–35 minutes

Cauliflower Pachadi

This is a traditional dish from Kerala in southern India, in which cauliflower is marinated in buttermilk before cooking.

- 375 g/12 oz cauliflower florets
- 150 ml/¼ pint buttermilk
- 1 teaspoon salt
- 3 tablespoons ghee
- 1 large onion, thinly sliced
- 2 garlic cloves, crushed
- 1 tablespoon freshly grated root ginger
- 1 teaspoon yellow mustard seeds
- 1 teaspoon black mustard seeds
- 1 teaspoon turmeric
- 25 g/1 oz desiccated coconut
- 150 ml/¼ pint water
- 2 tablespoons chopped fresh coriander
- pepper

1 Place the cauliflower florets in a bowl with the buttermilk, salt and some pepper. Mix well to combine the ingredients then cover and set aside for 2 hours to allow the cauliflower to marinate.

2 Heat the ghee in a heavy-based saucepan, add the onion, garlic and ginger and fry over gentle heat, stirring occasionally, for about 8 minutes until softened and lightly golden.

3 Add the 2 types of mustard seeds, the turmeric and coconut and cook for 3 minutes, stirring constantly.

4 Stir in the cauliflower with its buttermilk marinade and the water. Bring the curry to the boil, then reduce the heat, cover the pan and simmer gently for 12 minutes or until the cauliflower is tender.

5 Remove the lid, taste and adjust the seasoning if necessary and stir in the chopped coriander. Increase the heat and cook for a further 3–4 minutes to thicken the sauce. Serve hot as an accompaniment to other curries, with steamed rice or naan bread.

Serves 4
Preparation time: about 10 minutes, plus marinating
Cooking time: about 30 minutes

Aloo Gobi

Potatoes and cauliflower are both available in India, although they tend to be found only in the more temperate regions. Aloo Gobi is a good example of the way in which Indian cuisine has adapted itself to vegetables which have been introduced from other countries.

- 175 g/6 oz ghee
- 1 kg/2 lb potatoes, peeled and chopped into 2.5 cm/1 inch pieces
- 2 large onions, peeled and sliced
- 4 garlic cloves, peeled and sliced
- 2 teaspoons chilli powder
- 1 teaspoon ground turmeric
- 1 teaspoon ground coriander
- 2 teaspoons salt
- ½ teaspoon pepper
- 1.2 litres/2 pints water
- 500 g/1 lb cauliflower florets
- 2 teaspoons garam masala
- lime slices, to garnish (optional)

1 Melt the ghee in a large heavy-based pan, add the potatoes and fry gently for exactly 1 minute. Remove from the pan with a slotted spoon and set aside.
2 Add the onions and garlic to the pan and fry gently for about 5 minutes until soft. Add the chilli powder, turmeric, ground coriander, salt and pepper and fry for a further 3 minutes, stirring constantly.
3 Return the potatoes to the pan, add the water and bring to the boil. Lower the heat and simmer for 10 minutes.
4 Add the cauliflower and simmer for 15 minutes until the vegetables are tender and the sauce is thick.
5 Increase the heat to boil off any excess liquid if necessary. Stir in the garam masala, garnish with lime slices, if using, and serve hot.

Serves 4
Preparation time: 10 minutes
Cooking time: 30 minutes

Hot-tossed Cauliflower with Almonds

This recipe can be used for broccoli as well as cauliflower, with equally good results, and the almonds can be replaced with cashews or pine kernels, if you prefer.

- **1 medium cauliflower**
- **50 g/2 oz blanched almonds**
- **2 tablespoons vegetable oil**
- **1 onion, finely chopped**
- **2.5 cm/1 inch piece of fresh root ginger, peeled and finely chopped**
- **2 garlic cloves, crushed**
- **2 teaspoons ground coriander**
- **1 teaspoon turmeric**
- **½ teaspoon chilli powder**
- **75 ml/3 fl oz water**
- **salt**

1 Break the leaves off the cauliflower and reserve some of the small green leaves. Separate the florets from the stalks. Break the florets into individual sprigs and slice the stalks thinly on the diagonal. Blanch the stalks and sprigs in boiling salted water for 2 minutes. Drain, rinse immediately under cold running water and drain again.

2 Heat a wok until hot. Add the almonds and dry-fry over a gentle heat until toasted on all sides. Remove the wok from the heat and tip the toasted almonds on to a chopping board. Chop the almonds coarsely.

3 Return the wok to moderate heat.

Add the oil and heat until hot. Add the onion, ginger, garlic, ground coriander, turmeric and chilli powder and stir-fry for 2–3 minutes or until softened, taking care not to let any of the ingredients brown.

4 Add the cauliflower sprigs and stalks and sprinkle over the water and add salt to taste. Increase the heat to high and stir-fry for 2–3 minutes or until the cauliflower is tender but still crisp.

5 Taste and add more salt if necessary. Serve at once, sprinkled with the chopped toasted almonds and garnished with the reserved green cauliflower leaves.

Serves 4
Preparation time: 10 minutes
Cooking time: 10 minutes

Balti Courgettes

- 25 g/1 oz ghee or butter
- 1 small onion, chopped
- pinch of asafoetida (optional)
- 2 small potatoes, quartered
- 375 g/12 oz courgettes, sliced
- ½ teaspoon chilli powder
- ½ teaspoon ground turmeric
- 1 teaspoon ground coriander
- ½ teaspoon salt
- 150 ml/¼ pint water
- ½ teaspoon garam masala
- chopped fresh coriander, to garnish

1 Heat the ghee or butter in a Balti pan or heavy-based frying pan, add the onion and fry for 5 minutes, stirring occasionally, until softened.
2 Add the asafoetida, if using, then add the potatoes and fry for about 2–3 minutes.
3 Stir in the sliced courgettes, the chilli powder, turmeric, coriander and salt. Add the water, cover the pan and cook gently for 8–10 minutes until the potatoes are tender. Sprinkle with the garam masala and garnish with chopped coriander leaves. Serve at once with an Indian bread.

Serves 4
Preparation time: 10 minutes
Cooking time: about 15 minutes

Braised Okra with Chillies

- 50 g/2 oz ghee or butter
- 1 large onion, sliced
- 3 garlic cloves, sliced
- 5 cm/2 inch piece fresh root ginger, peeled and finely chopped
- 2 fresh green chillies, deseeded and finely chopped
- ½ teaspoon chilli powder
- 500 g/1 lb okra, trimmed
- 200 ml/7 fl oz water
- 2 teaspoons desiccated coconut
- salt

1 Melt the ghee or butter in a large wok or heavy-based saucepan, add the onion, garlic, ginger, chillies and chilli powder and fry gently for 4–5 minutes until soft, stirring occasionally.

2 Add the okra, water and salt to taste. Bring to the boil, then lower the heat, cover and simmer for 5–10 minutes until the okra are just tender but still firm to the bite. Stir in the coconut and serve hot.

Serves 4
Preparation time: 15 minutes
Cooking time: about 15 minutes

Aubergine Petjal

The English translation for this Indonesian dish is Aubergine and Peanut Curry. It goes very well with the Indonesian Spiced Coconut Rice on page 82. Sambal oelek is a very hot sauce made from chillies and vinegar so use it sparingly.

- ½ teaspoon salt
- 750 g/1½ lb aubergines, cut into 2.5 cm/ 1 inch cubes
- 3 tablespoons groundnut oil
- 4 shallots, chopped
- 2 garlic cloves, crushed
- 1 teaspoon dried shrimp paste
- ½ teaspoon ground galangal (laos powder)
- 250 ml/8 fl oz coconut milk (see page 7)
- 1 teaspoon tamarind paste
- 1 tablespoon dark soy sauce
- 1 tablespoon sambal oelek
- 1 tablespoon palm sugar or soft brown sugar
- 125 g/4 oz roasted peanuts, coarsely ground

1 Rub the salt all over the aubergine cubes and place them in a steamer above a pan of boiling water. Steam for about 5 minutes until just tender. Drain and set aside.

2 Heat the oil in a wok, add the shallots and garlic, and fry over a gentle heat, stirring frequently, for about 5 minutes or until softened. Add the shrimp paste and galangal (laos) powder and fry for 3 minutes.

3 Add the coconut milk, tamarind paste, soy sauce, sambal oelek and sugar. Stir well and simmer gently for 3 minutes. Stir the steamed aubergine into the sauce and cook gently for a further 5 minutes. Add the ground peanuts to the curry and cook gently for 2 minutes.

4 Serve immediately with rice.

Serves 6
Preparation time: about 10 minutes
Cooking time: 25 minutes

Rice, Breads, Side Dishes and Chutneys

Indonesian Spiced Coconut Rice

375 g/12 oz basmati rice

125 g/4 oz creamed coconut, chopped

7 cm/3 inch piece of lemon grass,
halved lengthways

5 cm/2 inch piece of cinnamon stick,
broken in half

4 curry leaves

½ teaspoon ground nutmeg

¼ teaspoon ground cloves

1 teaspoon salt

pinch of pepper

1 Place the rice in a sieve and wash it thoroughly under cold water. Drain and place in a large heavy-based saucepan. Dissolve the creamed coconut in 750 ml/1¼ pints boiling water. Add the coconut milk to the rice with the lemon grass, cinnamon, curry leaves, nutmeg, cloves and salt and pepper.

2 Bring the rice to the boil and then boil, uncovered, over moderate heat for 8 minutes, stirring frequently, until almost all the liquid is absorbed.

3 Reduce the heat to low, cover the pan with a tightly fitting lid and cook the rice very gently for a further 10 minutes.

4 Remove the pan from the heat and, working quickly, loosen the rice grains with a fork. Cover the pan with a clean, dry tea towel and allow the rice to cook in its own heat for a further 15 minutes. Serve immediately.

Serves 6

Preparation time: 5 minutes

Cooking time: 35 minutes

Chapati

- 250 g/8 oz wholemeal flour
- 1 teaspoon salt
- about 200 ml/⅓ pint water
- ghee or oil, for frying

1 Place the flour and salt in a bowl. Make a well in the centre, then gradually stir in the water and work to a soft, supple dough. Knead for 10 minutes, then cover and leave in a cool place for 30 minutes.
2 Knead again very thoroughly, then divide the dough into 12 pieces. Roll out each piece on a floured surface into a thin round pancake.
3 Lightly grease a griddle or heavy-based frying pan with a little ghee or oil and place over moderate heat. Add a chapati and cook until blisters appear. Press down with a fish slice, then turn and cook the other side until lightly coloured. Remove from the pan and keep warm while cooking the rest.
4 Brush a little butter on one side and serve warm as soon as possible.

Makes 12
Preparation time: 30 minutes, plus standing
Cooking time: 12 minutes

Paratha

Parathas are essentially fried chapatis. They are very filling, so only allow about 1½ per person. They are shown on the left of the picture.

- 250 g/8 oz wholemeal flour
- 1 teaspoon salt
- about 200 ml/⅓ pint water
- 50–75 g/2–3 oz melted ghee or butter

1 Make the dough as for Chapati (see left) and divide into 6 pieces. Roll out each piece on a floured surface into a thin circle. Brush with melted ghee or butter and fold in half; brush again and fold in half again. Roll out again to a circle about 3 mm/⅛ inch thick.
2 Lightly grease a griddle or heavy-based frying pan with a little ghee or butter and place over moderate heat. Add a paratha and cook for 1 minute. Lightly brush the top with a little ghee or butter and turn over. Brush all round the edge with ghee or butter and cook until golden. Remove from the pan and keep warm while cooking the rest. Serve hot.

Makes 6
Preparation time: 30 minutes
Cooking time: 15 minutes

Puri

A traditional Indian breakfast often includes this deep-fried bread served with a selection of chutneys.

- **250 g/8 oz plain wholemeal flour**
- **½ teaspoon salt**
- **about 125–175 ml/4–6 fl oz water**
- **vegetable oil, for deep-frying**

1 Sift the flour and salt into a bowl and make a well in the centre. Gradually add just enough water to make a dough. Knead well for 5–10 minutes, cover with a damp tea towel and set aside for about 30 minutes.

2 Divide the dough into 12–14 pieces. Working on a lightly floured surface roll out each piece of dough into a flat 7 cm/ 3 inch round.

3 Heat the oil in a large saucepan to 180–190°C (350–375°F), or until a cube of bread browns in 30 seconds. Slide in one puri at a time and fry on both sides until golden brown. It will quickly swell up in the oil.

4 Lift out the puri with a slotted spoon, and drain on kitchen paper. Continue frying the puris and stack in layers, alternating the thin and thick sides to prevent them sticking. Keep wrapped in a clean tea towel or place in a covered container while you fry the remaining puris. Serve hot.

Makes 12–14
Preparation time: 20 minutes, plus standing
Cooking time: about 30 minutes

Naan

- 15 g/½ oz fresh yeast
- ¼ teaspoon sugar
- 2 tablespoons warm water
- 500 g/1 lb self-raising flour
- 1 teaspoon salt
- 150 ml/¼ pint tepid milk
- 150 ml/¼ pint natural yogurt (at room temperature)
- 2 tablespoons melted butter or cooking oil

TO GARNISH:

- 2–3 tablespoons melted butter
- 1 tablespoon poppy or sesame seeds

1 Put the yeast into a small bowl with the sugar and water. Mix well until the yeast has dissolved, then leave in a warm place for 15 minutes or until the mixture is frothy.

2 Sift the flour and salt into a large bowl. Make a well in the centre and pour in the yeast, milk, yogurt and butter or oil. Mix well to a smooth dough and turn on to a floured surface. Knead well for about 10 minutes, until smooth and elastic.

3 Place in a bowl, cover with clingfilm and leave to rise in a warm place for 1–1½ hours, or until doubled in size.

4 Turn the dough on to a floured surface, knead for a few minutes, then divide into 6 pieces. Pat or roll each piece into a round.

5 Place on a warmed baking sheet and bake in a preheated oven, 240°C (475°F), Gas Mark 9, for 10 minutes.

6 Brush the naans with butter and sprinkle with the poppy or sesame seeds. Serve warm.

Makes 6

Preparation time: about 45 minutes, plus standing and rising
Cooking time: 10 minutes
Oven temperature: 240°C (475°F), Gas Mark 9

Kachori

- 250 g/8 oz plain wholemeal flour
- ½ teaspoon salt
- about 125–175 ml/4–6 fl oz water

FILLING:

- 50 g/2 oz lentils, washed and soaked for 3 hours
- ½ teaspoon cumin seeds
- ½ teaspoon aniseed
- 1–2 tablespoons vegetable oil
- pinch of asafoetida (optional)
- 1 small fresh green chilli, deseeded and very finely chopped, or ½ teaspoon chilli powder
- pinch of salt
- vegetable oil, for deep-frying

TO GARNISH:

- onion slices
- lime rings
- coriander, chopped

1 Sift the flour and salt and make a well in the centre. Gradually add just enough water to make a dough. Knead well for 5–10 minutes, then cover with a damp tea towel and set aside.

2 To make the filling, drain the lentils and grind to a thick, coarse paste with a little water. Heat a wok or heavy-based frying pan, add the cumin seeds and aniseeds and dry-fry for 30 seconds then grind coarsely. Heat 1 tablespoon of oil in the wok and sprinkle in the asafoetida, if using, and the lentil paste. Add the chilli or chilli powder and salt. Fry for 5 minutes, adding a little more oil if necessary. Leave to cool.

3 Divide the dough into 12–14 pieces. Roll each piece into a ball and make a depression in the middle. Press about 1 teaspoon of filling into the depression and reshape the dough into a ball, encircling the filling. Carefully roll out into a 7 cm/3 inch round.

4 Heat 5–6 cm/2–2½ inches of oil in a large saucepan and fry the kachoris a few at a time until golden brown on both sides. Remove with a slotted spoon and drain on kitchen paper. Keep warm while frying the remaining kachoris. Serve hot with a chutney.

Makes 12–14

Preparation time: 30 minutes, plus soaking
Cooking time: about 30 minutes

Pilau Rice

- 3 tablespoons oil
- 5 cm/2 inch piece of cinnamon stick
- 4 cardamom pods
- 4 cloves
- 1 onion, sliced
- 250 g/8 oz basmati rice, washed and soaked for 30 minutes
- 600 ml/1 pint beef stock or water
- salt
- fried onion rings (see page 8), to serve (optional)

1 Heat the oil in a large heavy-based saucepan, add the cinnamon, cardamom and cloves and fry for a few seconds. Add the sliced onion and fry until golden.

2 Drain the rice thoroughly, add to the pan and fry, stirring occasionally, for 5 minutes.

3 Add the stock or water and season to taste with salt. Bring to the boil, then simmer, uncovered, for 10 minutes until the rice is tender and the liquid absorbed. To serve, garnish with fried onion rings, if liked.

Serves 4
Preparation time: 10 minutes, plus soaking
Cooking time: about 20 minutes

VARIATION

Vegetable Pilau

Add 125 g/4 oz each shelled peas, thinly sliced carrots and cauliflower florets to the pan after frying the onion. Fry for 5 minutes, then add the rice and proceed as in the main recipe.

Pineapple Chutney

Try this tangy chutney as an unusual alternative to classic mango chutney.

- 1 large, ripe pineapple, peeled, cored and chopped into small pieces
- 3 shallots, chopped
- 1 green chilli, deseeded and finely chopped
- 1 tablespoon finely chopped fresh root ginger
- 25 g/1 oz raisins
- 125 g/4 oz soft brown sugar
- 125 ml/4 fl oz distilled malt vinegar
- ¼ teaspoon salt

1 Place the pineapple in a heavy-based saucepan with the shallots, chilli, ginger, raisins, sugar, vinegar and salt. Cook over moderate heat, stirring constantly, until the sugar has dissolved. Bring the mixture to the boil, then reduce the heat a little and cook on a steady boil for 8–10 minutes, stirring occasionally, until most of the liquid has evaporated and the chutney is thick.

2 Pour the hot chutney into sterilized jars, seal, label and store. Once opened the chutney will keep well for 3–4 weeks in the refrigerator. Serve with poppadums or as an accompaniment to curries.

Makes about 475 g/15 oz chutney
Preparation time: 10 minutes
Cooking time: 15 minutes

Mango Chutney

The concentrated flavour of dried mangoes makes this a particularly fruity-tasting chutney. It can be stored in a cool place for up to 2–3 months.

- 250 g/8 oz dried mangoes, soaked in cold water overnight
- 1 teaspoon chilli powder
- 6 cardamom pods, bruised
- 3 cloves
- 1 teaspoon black mustard seeds
- 1 teaspoon coriander seeds, lightly crushed
- 5 black peppercorns, lightly crushed
- 1 small cinnamon stick, broken in half
- 375 g/12 oz fresh mango flesh, cut into 1 cm/1½ inch cubes
- 1 large garlic clove, sliced thinly
- ½ teaspoon salt
- 300 ml/½ pint white wine vinegar
- 375 g/12 oz caster sugar

1 Drain the dried mangoes, reserving 300 ml/½ pint of the soaking liquid and cut into 1.5 cm/¾ inch pieces.

2 Place the chilli powder, cardamom pods, cloves, mustard seeds, coriander seeds, peppercorns and cinnamon stick in a large heavy-based saucepan. Dry-fry the spices over gentle heat, stirring frequently, for 2–3 minutes until fragrant.

3 Add the reserved mango soaking liquid, the chopped dried and the fresh mangoes, the garlic, salt and vinegar to the spices. Bring the mixture to the boil, then reduce the heat and simmer gently for 10 minutes, stirring occasionally.

4 Add the sugar and stir over a gentle heat until it has dissolved. Raise the heat and boil the chutney, stirring frequently, until it is thick. This will take about 40 minutes.

5 Ladle the chutney into sterilized jars, seal, label and store.

Makes about 1 kg/2 lb chutney
Preparation time: 20 minutes, plus overnight soaking
Cooking time: 55 minutes

Papaya and Coriander Raita

This cooling accompaniment can be made with fresh mango instead of the papaya.

- 175 g/6 oz natural yogurt
- ½ ripe papaya, peeled, deseeded and diced
- 2 tablespoons chopped fresh coriander
- ½ teaspoon finely grated lime zest
- 1 teaspoon lime juice (or more, according to taste)
- salt

1 Place the yogurt, papaya, coriander, lime zest and juice in a bowl; season with salt and mix gently to combine. Taste and adjust the seasoning, adding more lime juice if liked.
2 Cover the raita and leave in the refrigerator for 30 minutes before serving to allow all the flavours to develop. Serve with curries or as a dip.

Serves 4
Preparation time: 10 minutes, plus chilling

Cucumber and Mint Raita

This refreshing raita goes particularly well with lamb dishes.

- 175 g/6 oz natural yogurt
- 75 g/3 oz cucumber, cut into matchstick strips
- 2 tablespoons chopped fresh mint
- pinch of ground cumin
- lemon juice, to taste
- salt

1 Place the yogurt, cucumber and mint in a bowl. Add the cumin and lemon juice to taste and season with a little salt.

2 Cover the bowl and leave in the refrigerator for at least 30 minutes before serving to allow all the flavours to develop.

Serves 4
Preparation time: 10 minutes, plus chilling

VARIATION

Banana and Coconut Raita

For a cooling raita to serve with hot curries from southern India and other parts of the tropics, omit the cucumber, mint and cumin. Add 2 small thinly sliced bananas, 2 tablespoons toasted desiccated coconut and a pinch of chilli powder to the yogurt and stir gently to mix. Add lemon juice to taste and season with salt. Serve immediately.

Green Bean Sambal

This sambal makes a very good accompaniment to both Indonesian and Malaysian curries.

- 2 tablespoons vegetable oil
- 4 shallots, thinly sliced
- 2 garlic cloves, crushed
- ¼ teaspoon shrimp paste
- 250 g/8 oz French beans, topped, tailed and sliced thinly on an acute angle
- 2 teaspoons sambal oelek (hot pepper condiment)
- 1 teaspoon soft brown sugar
- salt

1 Heat the oil in a frying pan, add the shallots, garlic and shrimp paste and fry over a low heat, stirring frequently, for 5 minutes until the shallots are softened.

2 Add the beans, increase the heat to moderate and fry, stirring occasionally, for 8 minutes, until the beans are cooked but not too soft.

3 Stir in the sambal oelek, sugar and a little salt and continue frying the beans for 1 further minute. Taste and add a little more salt if necessary. Serve the sambal hot.

Serves 4
Preparation time: 15 minutes
Cooking time: 15 minutes

Recipe photographers:
Reed International Books Ltd./
Jeremy Hopley/Graham Kirk/
James Murphy/Alan Newnham/
Charlie Stebbings
Jacket Photographer:
Graham Kirk
Jacket Home Economist:
Sunil Vijayaker